Copyright © 2024 Andrea Oliver

All rights reserved

The characters and events portrayed in this book are fictitious. Any similarity to real persons, living or dead, is coincidental and not intended by the author.

No part of this book may be reproduced, or stored in a retrieval system, or transmitted in any form or by any means, electronic, mechanical, photocopying, recording, or otherwise, without express written permission of the publisher.

Cover design by: Art Painter
Library of Congress Control Number: 2018675309
Printed in the United States of America

CONTENTS

Copyright

Introduction: The Power of Organic Marketing for Small Businesses … 2

Chapter 1: Understanding the Basics of Organic Marketing … 11

Chapter 2: Crafting a Winning Organic Marketing Strategy … 23

Chapter 3: Developing an Effective Content Strategy … 33

Chapter 4: Mastering Social Media for Organic Growth … 47

Chapter 5: SEO—Driving Organic Traffic to Your Website … 65

Chapter 6: Email Marketing—Nurturing Relationships Organically … 76

Chapter 7: Leveraging Online Communities and Forums … 90

Chapter 8: Building Partnerships and Collaborations … 98

Chapter 9: Analyzing and Measuring Your Organic Marketing Success … 106

Chapter 10: Scaling Your Organic Marketing Over Time … 115

ANDREA OLIVER

Organic Marketing Guide for Small Businesses

INTRODUCTION: THE POWER OF ORGANIC MARKETING FOR SMALL BUSINESSES

Welcome to the **Organic Marketing Guide for Small Businesses**! You're about to embark on a journey to discover how to grow your business using organic marketing methods—strategies that don't require huge ad budgets but still deliver powerful, long-lasting results.

Organic marketing is all about building meaningful, authentic connections with your audience. It's a slower, more intentional process compared to paid ads, but the beauty of it is that once you lay the groundwork, the results compound over time. Think of it like planting a garden: you nurture it consistently, and in return, it provides fruits for years to come. For small businesses with limited budgets, this approach is not just smart; it's essential.

What is Organic Marketing?

Organic marketing refers to all the efforts you make to promote your business **without paying for ads**. It includes everything from creating valuable content, engaging with your community, optimizing your website for search engines, to networking at local events. It's the art of leveraging your resources and creativity to grow your business through unpaid channels.

But don't mistake "unpaid" for "free." Organic marketing still takes time, effort, and a well-thought-out strategy. It's not about just throwing up a few social media posts and hoping for the best. It's about **being strategic** with your time and resources to build relationships, trust, and ultimately, a loyal customer base.

Why is Organic Marketing Important for Small Businesses?

If you're a small business owner, you know that every dollar counts. Large companies can afford to throw millions at paid advertising to attract customers, but small businesses need to be more resourceful. Organic marketing allows you to grow **without the financial risk** of paid campaigns.

For small businesses, the trust factor is key. When people see your brand engaging with them authentically—answering questions on social media, sharing valuable blog posts, or showing up at local events—they trust you more. And trust leads to sales.

Moreover, organic strategies build a **long-term foundation** for your business. Instead of constantly relying on paid ads to bring in new customers, organic marketing sets up a system where customers naturally find you and stay with you because they believe in your brand. That means more **repeat business, word-of-mouth referrals, and customer loyalty**.

The Key Benefits of Organic Marketing

There are many reasons to embrace organic marketing, but

let's highlight a few major ones that make it a no-brainer for small businesses:

1. **Cost-Effective**: You don't need a big advertising budget to be successful. Instead, you invest time and effort in building something that will continue to work for you in the long term.
2. **Builds Trust and Authority**: Organic marketing strategies, such as content creation and social media engagement, help position you as an expert in your industry. The more value you provide without asking for anything in return, the more people trust you. Trust turns into brand loyalty, which turns into repeat business and word-of-mouth referrals.
3. **Sustainable Long-Term Growth**: Unlike paid ads, which stop delivering once your budget runs out, organic marketing keeps working for you long after the initial effort is made. A well-written blog post can drive traffic to your website for years. A strong social media presence continues to grow as your followers share your content.
4. **Encourages Meaningful Engagement**: Organic marketing is all about building relationships. Whether you're replying to comments on Instagram or engaging with your community through a local event, organic strategies are interactive. They encourage conversations that build a loyal, engaged customer base.
5. **Brand Authenticity**: In an age where people are wary of being "sold to," organic marketing feels more genuine. When you provide helpful content, offer real value, and engage with customers

authentically, you're not just trying to make a sale—you're building relationships. This authenticity helps your brand stand out in a sea of companies pushing paid ads.

How Organic Marketing Drives Long-Term Growth

If you're looking for **overnight success**, organic marketing isn't the quick-fix solution. But if you're in this for the long haul—and most small business owners are—organic marketing offers long-term growth that's both sustainable and powerful.

Here's why:

1. **Compound Effect**: One of the greatest strengths of organic marketing is its compounding nature. When you publish a blog post, it doesn't just drive traffic that day. It continues to rank on search engines and bring people to your website for months or even years. The same goes for building a strong social media following or email list—your efforts accumulate over time.
2. **Evergreen Content**: Unlike a Facebook ad that has a shelf life of a few days or weeks, organic marketing efforts (like creating evergreen content) continue to work for you long after they're published. Evergreen content refers to articles, videos, or resources that remain relevant over time. For example, a "How to Start a Small Business" guide will always be valuable to your target audience, no matter when they discover it.
3. **Building a Loyal Audience**: Organic marketing

builds relationships, not just transactions. By engaging with your audience consistently, you create a community of loyal customers who will keep coming back to you. This loyalty is worth far more than a one-time sale.
4. **Reduced Dependency on Paid Ads**: Relying too heavily on paid advertising is risky because once your ad budget runs dry, so does your traffic. Organic marketing doesn't have this problem. By using long-term strategies, you decrease your dependency on paid channels and focus on sustainable growth.

Examples of Organic Marketing in Action

Let's look at a few examples of small businesses that have grown organically using these strategies:

Case Study 1: A Local Bakery's Social Media Success

One of the most powerful organic marketing success stories comes from a local bakery in Brooklyn, New York. When the bakery first opened, the owners didn't have the budget for paid ads, but they knew they needed to get the word out fast.

Here's what they did:

- **Instagram as the Main Platform**: The bakery started an Instagram page where they posted daily pictures of their pastries and behind-the-scenes videos of their baking process. The posts didn't just promote their products—they engaged with the community by asking followers for feedback on new recipes and sharing customer stories.
- **Consistency**: Every day, the bakery posted some-

thing new. They built up anticipation by previewing their daily specials and even gave their followers a say in what should be on the menu. This generated a lot of engagement and made their followers feel like they were part of the bakery's journey.
- **Local Influencer Collaboration**: They reached out to local food bloggers and influencers, offering them free pastries in exchange for a review or shout-out on their social channels. This helped them grow their following organically as influencers' audiences discovered the bakery.

The result? Within six months, the bakery had over 10,000 Instagram followers and their shop was regularly packed with customers. The buzz they built online directly translated to foot traffic, without spending a single dollar on ads.

Case Study 2: The Power of Blogging for a Home Decor Business

A home decor business, run by a couple out of their garage, used **content marketing** to grow their business. When they started, they didn't have the resources for a flashy website or paid ads, but they knew they could write.

Here's what they did:

- **Blogging for SEO**: They started a blog on their website, writing weekly articles on topics like DIY home decor projects, styling tips, and furniture restoration tutorials. Their content wasn't just a way to promote their products—it was a way to provide value to people interested in home decor.
- **Keyword Research**: They used free SEO tools to find out what keywords their target audience was

searching for and optimized their blog posts accordingly. By targeting long-tail keywords (specific phrases with lower competition), they were able to rank on the first page of Google for several key search terms.
- **Organic Social Media Promotion**: Every time they published a blog post, they shared it across their social media channels, Pinterest in particular. They also encouraged their readers to share the content, which led to more traffic.

Within a year, their blog was driving 80% of their website's traffic, and their small business started receiving national attention from media outlets that discovered them through their content.

Case Study 3: Local Networking for a Freelance Graphic Designer

Freelancers and solopreneurs can also benefit immensely from organic marketing. One graphic designer in Austin, Texas, used **local networking** to grow her client base entirely through word-of-mouth.

Here's what she did:

- **Local Meetups**: She joined local business and entrepreneur meetups, where she made personal connections with small business owners who needed design work. At every event, she handed out business cards and followed up with people she met.
- **Workshops and Speaking Events**: She offered free graphic design workshops at co-working spaces and libraries, teaching small business owners basic design principles. These workshops not only

established her as an expert in her field but also generated leads—many attendees ended up hiring her for more advanced design projects.
- **Partnerships**: She partnered with a local marketing agency, offering to provide design services to their clients. In return, the agency recommended her to their network of small business owners.

Through these organic efforts, she built a steady client base without spending anything on paid advertising. Her referrals continued to grow, and soon, she had more work than she could handle.

What You'll Learn in This Guide

This guide is packed with actionable strategies and insights to help you replicate the success of businesses like the ones you've just read about. Whether you're running a bakery, a home decor shop, or a freelance business, the organic marketing strategies in this book can be tailored to your unique needs.

Here's a quick overview of what you'll learn:

1. **How to Develop a Strong Online Presence**: From optimizing your website for search engines to creating engaging social media content, you'll learn how to build a digital presence that attracts customers organically.
2. **Content Marketing and SEO**: You'll discover how to create content that ranks on Google, drives traffic to your website, and converts visitors into customers—all without paying for ads.
3. **Email Marketing and Community Building**:

Learn how to grow your email list, nurture your subscribers, and create an engaged community around your brand.
4. **Real-World Marketing**: We'll dive into the power of word-of-mouth marketing, local networking, and partnerships to grow your business offline.
5. **Bridging Online and Offline Efforts**: Finally, we'll show you how to seamlessly integrate your online and offline marketing efforts for maximum impact.

By the time you finish this book, you'll have a full arsenal of organic marketing strategies that you can start using today to grow your business. Whether you're just starting out or looking to take your business to the next level, these methods are designed to work for **any small business**.

Let's get started on building the foundation for your business's long-term success—without relying on expensive ad campaigns!

CHAPTER 1: UNDERSTANDING THE BASICS OF ORGANIC MARKETING

Welcome to the first chapter of your journey toward mastering organic marketing for small businesses. Whether you're a solo entrepreneur or managing a small team, the principles and strategies you're about to learn will transform how you approach growth and customer acquisition. Organic marketing doesn't require massive budgets or complex systems—it's all about being resourceful, authentic, and strategic. You've already got what it takes; now, it's time to maximize those efforts.

Let's start by defining what organic marketing is, why it's so effective for small businesses, and how you can start leveraging it today to build long-term success.

What is Organic Marketing?

Organic marketing is the process of using unpaid strategies to attract, engage, and convert customers. It's all about **naturally drawing people** to your brand by creating valuable content, building genuine relationships, and fostering community engagement. It involves **earned attention**, meaning your audience finds you through content that's valuable to them, rather than by clicking on paid advertisements.

Imagine organic marketing like planting a seed. You nurture it with consistent care, and over time, it grows roots deep into the ground. When you invest effort into organic marketing, it builds **momentum**—your brand's visibility increases, customer trust grows, and eventually, people start seeking you out without you having to chase them down.

Here are some key components of organic marketing:

- **Content creation**: Blogging, videos, podcasts, infographics—anything that educates, inspires, or solves problems for your audience.
- **Social media engagement**: Building a loyal following by sharing value-driven content, engaging in conversations, and fostering community.
- **Search engine optimization (SEO)**: Optimizing your website and content to appear in search engine results when potential customers search for related topics.
- **Email marketing**: Nurturing relationships with leads and customers through personalized, value-driven communication.

When done correctly, organic marketing helps you grow in a **sustainable** way. It takes time and effort, but the results build on themselves. A single blog post can bring traffic to your site for years, and one happy customer can refer countless others over time.

Why is it Called "Organic" Marketing?

The term "organic" refers to the natural, **non-paid** nature of these strategies. You're not paying for visibility; instead, you're earning it. This differs from paid marketing, where you essentially buy attention through advertising. In organic marketing, your growth comes from the **value** you offer, the relationships you build, and the reputation you establish.

Think of it like word-of-mouth—one person has a great experience with your business and tells their friends. Except, with organic marketing, you're doing this at scale, using digital platforms to expand your reach and influence.

Differences Between Organic and Paid Marketing

Before diving into the nuts and bolts of organic marketing, it's essential to understand how it compares to **paid marketing**. While both approaches can play a role in your overall strategy, they serve different purposes, and each has its own strengths and weaknesses.

Paid Marketing: Quick Wins, Short-Term Results

Paid marketing involves purchasing ad space, whether that's through Google, Facebook, Instagram, or other platforms. These ads are designed to **quickly grab attention**, driving traffic, leads, or sales in a relatively short time frame. Think of it like a tap: you pay to turn it on, and when you stop paying, the flow of leads stops as well.

Some key points about paid marketing:

- **Fast results**: With a well-targeted ad campaign, you can see immediate traffic and conversions.
- **Controlled targeting**: Paid ads allow you to laser-focus on specific demographics, interests, and behaviors, ensuring your content is seen by the right

people.
- **Cost**: The downside is that you're paying for every click, impression, or conversion. Once your budget runs out, the exposure stops.
- **Temporary**: Paid marketing is a short-term play. Ads work while they're running, but they don't create lasting impact unless continuously funded.

For small businesses with limited budgets, relying too heavily on paid marketing can be risky. It's effective, but expensive, and often doesn't leave a lasting mark.

Organic Marketing: Building a Sustainable Presence

Organic marketing, on the other hand, is more like playing the long game. It takes longer to see results, but those results are **long-lasting**. A blog post optimized for SEO can bring in traffic for years. A loyal social media following will continue engaging with your content and even spread it on your behalf. Organic marketing builds a **foundation** that paid ads simply can't.

Here's how organic marketing differs:

- **Slow but steady**: Organic strategies take time to build momentum, but they create ongoing value that doesn't disappear once you stop funding it.
- **Low-cost**: While organic marketing does require time and effort, it doesn't require large budgets. You can implement most strategies with little to no upfront cost.
- **Trust-building**: People trust organic content more than paid ads. Think about it—when you search for something online, do you click on the paid ads or the organic results? Most people skip the ads and head straight for the **organic listings**

because they perceive them as more credible and unbiased.
- **Relationship-focused**: Organic marketing is about fostering genuine relationships with your audience, building trust, and encouraging **brand loyalty**.

While paid marketing can give you a quick boost, organic marketing creates **lasting results**. The two can complement each other—perhaps using paid ads to jumpstart traffic while your organic efforts take root—but for small businesses on a budget, focusing on organic strategies provides **long-term value**.

The Long-Term Benefits of Organic Growth: Trust, Engagement, and Brand Loyalty

One of the most powerful aspects of organic marketing is its ability to build **trust**. Trust is the foundation of any successful business, especially for small businesses where relationships are key to growth.

1. Building Trust

When people find your brand through organic channels, they're more likely to view you as an **authority** in your field. Whether it's discovering your business through a Google search, reading an insightful blog post, or engaging with you on social media, the organic nature of their discovery makes them feel more **connected** to you.

Unlike paid ads, which often feel intrusive or "salesy," organic marketing is about **providing value**. You're not pushing your product in front of people; you're inviting them to engage with your brand by solving their problems, answering their questions, and offering helpful resources. This creates an **authentic connection**.

Think of organic marketing like building a friendship. You wouldn't trust a stranger who knocked on your door and immediately tried to sell you something, but you might trust someone who spent time getting to know you, understanding your needs, and offering solutions.

Case Study: Building Trust with Content

Let's look at a small local coffee shop that wanted to expand its presence beyond foot traffic and into online sales for coffee beans and merchandise. Instead of launching an expensive paid ad campaign, they started a **content marketing strategy** focused on sharing their knowledge of coffee.

They created blog posts on topics like:

- How to brew the perfect cup of coffee at home.
- The health benefits of drinking coffee.
- Behind-the-scenes stories about sourcing their beans from sustainable farms.

They also filmed short videos showing baristas demonstrating different brewing techniques, which they shared on their social media platforms. By offering **valuable content** to coffee lovers, they positioned themselves as experts in their field, and customers started trusting them more. As a result, their online sales grew steadily, and they began receiving inquiries from new customers who had discovered them through Google searches or social media shares.

The key here is that they **earned trust** by providing helpful, relevant content that aligned with their customers' interests. And because this trust was built organically, it had a lasting impact.

2. Increasing Engagement

Engagement is the lifeblood of organic marketing. The more engaged your audience is, the more likely they are to become loyal customers who not only buy from you but also **advocate for your brand**.

Organic marketing thrives on building relationships. On social media, for example, you're not just broadcasting messages—you're starting conversations. When someone leaves a comment on your post, you respond. When someone asks a question, you answer thoughtfully. This kind of **authentic interaction** fosters deep connections with your audience.

Actionable Tip: How to Boost Engagement on Social Media

Let's say you're a small clothing boutique. Rather than just posting pictures of your latest items with a "buy now" call-to-action, try engaging your audience with posts like:

- "Which fall look is your favorite? Vote in the comments!"
- "Tag a friend who needs to see these new arrivals!"
- "What's your go-to cozy outfit for a chilly day?"

These kinds of posts encourage engagement and build relationships with your followers. Over time, these interactions lead to more meaningful connections and customer loyalty.

3. Fostering Brand Loyalty

Finally, one of the most significant long-term benefits of organic marketing is its ability to foster **brand loyalty**. When customers feel a connection to your brand—because they trust you and engage with your content regularly—they're far more likely to stick around and become repeat buyers.

Loyalty is critical for small businesses because it's far more cost-effective to retain existing customers than to acquire new ones. Plus, loyal customers are your best brand advocates. They tell their friends about you, leave glowing reviews, and even defend your brand online.

Case Study: Building Loyalty with a Personal Brand

Take the case of a freelance graphic designer who built her entire business through **organic social media marketing**. Instead of running ads, she focused on building a personal brand that connected with her ideal clients. She posted behind-the-scenes videos of her design process, shared tips for fellow freelancers, and consistently engaged with her followers by responding to every comment and message.

Over time, her followers became loyal fans who not only hired her for projects but also referred her to their networks. She built such a strong connection with her audience that she rarely had to "sell" herself—her followers did it for her.

The key to her success was building authentic relationships through organic marketing. By consistently showing up and offering value, she earned the trust and loyalty of her audience, leading to **steady, sustainable growth**.

Why Organic Marketing Matters for Small Businesses

For small businesses with limited budgets, organic marketing is not just a strategy—it's a **necessity**. You don't have the luxury of spending thousands of dollars a month on paid ads. Instead, you need to be resourceful, creative, and strategic with how you grow your business.

1. Cost-Effective Strategies for Limited Budgets

One of the most significant advantages of organic marketing is that it doesn't require large upfront investments. While paid ads can quickly drain your budget, organic strategies rely more on **time and effort** than money. This makes them ideal for small businesses operating on a shoestring budget.

For example:

- Writing a blog post costs nothing but time and can bring in traffic for months or even years.
- Posting consistently on social media builds your brand presence without paying for visibility.
- Sending personalized emails to your existing customers helps nurture relationships and increase repeat business without buying ads.

2. Building a Sustainable Brand Presence Over Time

While paid marketing is excellent for short-term bursts of traffic, it doesn't build the same lasting foundation as organic marketing. Once you stop paying for ads, the traffic stops. But with organic marketing, your efforts continue to pay off long after they're implemented.

Imagine creating a **how-to video** for your product that gains traction on YouTube. That video could continue to bring in views and customers for years, even if you never promote it again. Similarly, a well-optimized blog post can drive organic traffic to your website for months after it's published.

For small businesses looking to build a sustainable presence, organic marketing is the way to go.

Common Organic Marketing Channels

Now that we've covered the benefits, let's dive into some of the most effective channels for organic marketing. These are the platforms and tools you'll use to grow your brand without relying on paid advertising.

1. Social Media Platforms

Social media is one of the most powerful tools for organic marketing because it allows you to build and nurture relationships with your audience. Here's a quick overview of how to use the most popular platforms:

- **Facebook**: Best for building a community around your brand. Facebook Groups are particularly valuable for fostering engagement and creating a sense of belonging among your audience.
- **Instagram**: Perfect for visual storytelling. Use Instagram to showcase your products, share behind-the-scenes content, and engage with your audience through Stories, Reels, and comments.
- **LinkedIn**: Ideal for B2B marketing and professional networking. Use LinkedIn to share thought leadership content, connect with potential clients, and establish yourself as an expert in your field.
- **Twitter**: Great for real-time engagement and sharing quick updates. Twitter is perfect for businesses that want to stay on top of industry trends and engage in ongoing conversations with their audience.

2. Search Engine Optimization (SEO)

SEO is the process of optimizing your website and content

to rank higher in search engine results, making it easier for potential customers to find you. SEO involves both **on-page optimization** (like using the right keywords and improving your website's structure) and **off-page optimization** (like building backlinks from other reputable sites).

3. Content Marketing

Content marketing involves creating valuable, informative, or entertaining content that attracts your target audience. This can include blog posts, videos, podcasts, infographics, and more. The key is to provide content that addresses your audience's needs and interests, positioning your brand as a **helpful resource**.

4. Email Marketing

Email marketing is one of the most direct and personal ways to connect with your audience. By building an email list of customers and prospects, you can send personalized messages that nurture relationships and encourage repeat business. The best part? Email marketing is **highly cost-effective** and provides one of the highest returns on investment of any marketing strategy.

Action Steps to Get Started with Organic Marketing

Now that you understand the basics, here are a few actionable steps to start implementing organic marketing for your small business:

1. **Identify your target audience**: Before creating any content or engaging on social media, you need to know who you're trying to reach. What are their pain points, needs, and interests? The

more you understand your audience, the better you can tailor your organic marketing efforts to resonate with them.
2. **Create valuable content**: Start with one or two channels (such as blogging and Instagram) and focus on creating content that provides value to your audience. Don't try to be everywhere at once—pick the platforms where your audience spends the most time and start there.
3. **Engage with your audience**: Organic marketing isn't just about pushing out content—it's about creating conversations. Respond to comments, answer questions, and engage with your followers regularly to build relationships.
4. **Optimize for SEO**: If you have a website, make sure it's optimized for search engines. This means doing keyword research, improving site speed, and creating valuable content that answers your audience's questions.
5. **Be patient**: Remember, organic marketing takes time. You won't see results overnight, but with consistent effort, your brand will grow, and your audience will come to you.

Organic marketing is one of the most powerful tools for small businesses. It's not just about growing your customer base—it's about building a brand that people trust, engage with, and stay loyal to. By focusing on long-term strategies and providing real value to your audience, you can create a sustainable presence that leads to steady growth for years to come.

CHAPTER 2: CRAFTING A WINNING ORGANIC MARKETING STRATEGY

Welcome to the heart of building a successful business—**strategy**. Organic marketing isn't about throwing out random content and hoping it sticks. It's about intentionality, focus, and understanding your business goals, audience, and brand message. In this chapter, we're going to dig deep into what it takes to create an organic marketing strategy that aligns with your business goals and drives sustainable growth. Whether you're just starting out or refining your approach, this chapter will give you practical advice, examples, and actionable steps to get started.

You already know the importance of organic marketing; now let's create a blueprint to make it work for you.

Define Your Business Goals

Before you can jump into crafting content or engaging with your audience, you need to have a **clear vision** of what you're aiming to achieve. Without defined goals, your marketing efforts will lack direction, and you'll find it challenging to measure success or make necessary adjustments.

Defining your business goals is the foundation of your marketing strategy. This step ensures you're not just busy creating content and posting on social media, but rather working toward specific, measurable objectives that align with your business's growth.

Why Setting Goals is Critical

Think of your goals as a **roadmap**. Without them, you wouldn't know where you're heading or how to get there. When you set clear goals, you gain clarity, focus, and a sense of purpose that guides your marketing decisions. Plus, goals provide a way to **measure progress**. You'll be able to look back and see whether your efforts are producing the desired outcomes.

Your goals will likely fall into categories such as:

- Increasing brand awareness
- Driving website traffic
- Generating leads
- Converting leads into customers
- Building customer loyalty
- Growing your social media following

But setting vague goals like "I want more customers" isn't enough. You need to create goals that are actionable, realistic, and aligned with the growth you envision for your business.

Setting SMART Goals

One of the best ways to structure your business goals is by using the **SMART** framework. SMART goals are:

- **Specific**: Your goals should be clear and specific. What exactly do you want to achieve? For example, instead of saying "I want to grow my email list," say "I want to grow my email list by 500 sub-

scribers over the next three months."
- **Measurable**: You need to be able to track your progress. How will you measure success? For example, if your goal is to increase website traffic, decide how much traffic you want to drive each month and how you will track it (e.g., through Google Analytics).
- **Achievable**: Your goals should be realistic. While it's important to aim high, setting goals that are too ambitious can set you up for failure. Consider your resources, time, and current capabilities when setting goals.
- **Relevant**: Your goals should be directly related to your overall business objectives. For example, if your primary business goal is to increase online sales, your marketing goals should focus on driving traffic to your website and converting leads into buyers.
- **Time-bound**: Every goal should have a deadline. By when do you want to achieve your goal? Setting a timeframe adds a sense of urgency and helps you stay accountable.

Aligning Marketing Efforts with Business Objectives

Once your SMART goals are in place, you need to ensure your marketing efforts align with your broader **business objectives**. For example, if one of your business goals is to increase sales by 20% this year, your marketing strategy should focus on driving qualified traffic to your website and nurturing leads into paying customers. It's about understanding that marketing isn't an isolated activity—it's a key driver in achieving your company's overall success.

Let's look at a small retail business as an example. Let's say the business owner's goal is to boost online sales by 25%

within six months. To align their marketing strategy with this goal, they could focus on:

- Increasing website traffic through SEO and social media content.
- Engaging with followers on Instagram and Facebook to showcase their new product line.
- Sending targeted email campaigns to past customers with personalized offers.

This approach ensures that every marketing activity is focused on achieving that specific sales target.

Know Your Target Audience

Now that you have your goals set, it's time to talk about the most crucial part of your organic marketing strategy: **knowing your audience**. You can't market to everyone, and that's okay! The goal is to focus on a specific group of people who are most likely to engage with your content, buy your products, or use your services.

Understanding your target audience is about more than just demographics—it's about **understanding their needs, desires, pain points, and preferences**. It's about knowing what makes them tick, what problems they face, and how your product or service can help solve those problems.

Creating Detailed Customer Personas

The best way to get clear on who your audience is is by creating **customer personas** (sometimes called buyer personas). These are detailed profiles that represent your ideal customers. Think of them as fictional characters based on real data and insights about your target audience.

A well-crafted customer persona includes:

- **Demographics**: Age, gender, occupation, education, income level, location.
- **Psychographics**: Interests, values, lifestyle, opinions, personality traits.
- **Pain Points**: What challenges are they facing that your product or service can solve?
- **Goals**: What are their goals and how does your business help them achieve those goals?
- **Buying Behavior**: What motivates them to buy? How do they typically make purchasing decisions? Are they price-sensitive or do they prioritize quality?

Let's create a persona for a fitness studio targeting busy professionals. Meet "Jane":

- **Name**: Jane
- **Age**: 35
- **Occupation**: Marketing Manager
- **Income**: $70,000/year
- **Location**: Suburban city
- **Pain Points**: Jane struggles to find time for fitness due to her demanding job. She's tired and stressed by the end of the day, but she knows she needs to stay active for her health.
- **Goals**: Jane wants to find a fitness routine that is flexible with her schedule and provides mental clarity. She's looking for a supportive community that keeps her motivated.
- **Buying Behavior**: Jane values convenience and community. She's willing to pay a premium for services that save her time and fit her busy lifestyle.

By crafting detailed personas like Jane, you'll be able to create **tailored content** and **marketing messages** that resonate with your audience on a deeper level.

Understanding Customer Needs, Pain Points, and Preferences

Knowing your customer's pain points allows you to position your product or service as the **solution**. Let's go back to Jane, our busy marketing manager. Her biggest pain point is finding time for fitness. As the owner of a fitness studio, you could position your services in a way that addresses that pain point, such as offering short, high-intensity classes that fit into her schedule, or providing virtual classes she can join from home.

Another example is a small eCommerce business selling eco-friendly products. If you know that your target audience values sustainability, your marketing messages should emphasize how your products are environmentally friendly, ethically sourced, and contribute to a greener planet.

Actionable Step: Conduct Audience Research

The best way to get to know your audience is by doing research. Here are a few ways you can gather information about your target customers:

1. **Surveys**: Send out a survey to your existing customers to learn more about their preferences, needs, and challenges.
2. **Social Media Insights**: Use tools like Facebook Insights and Instagram Analytics to gather demographic data on your followers.
3. **Website Analytics**: Tools like Google Analytics

can help you understand who is visiting your website, how they found you, and what content resonates with them.
4. **Competitor Research**: Analyze who your competitors are targeting and what strategies they're using. This can help you identify gaps in the market or areas where you can differentiate.

The more you know about your audience, the more targeted and effective your marketing efforts will be.

Creating a Consistent Brand Message

Now that you have your goals set and you know who your audience is, the next step is crafting a **consistent brand message**. Your brand message is the story your business tells—it's the way you communicate your value, differentiate yourself from competitors, and build relationships with customers.

A strong brand message is more than just a tagline or slogan—it's about creating a unified voice and tone that resonates with your audience across all marketing channels.

Developing Your Unique Selling Proposition (USP)

Your **unique selling proposition** (USP) is the key element that differentiates your business from others in the market. It's what makes you stand out. Your USP could be anything from offering the fastest service in your industry to providing a product that no one else has.

To develop your USP, ask yourself:

- What makes your product or service unique?
- What benefits do you offer that your competitors

don't?
- Why should customers choose you over someone else?

Let's look at a small organic skincare brand as an example. Their USP could be that they use only 100% organic ingredients sourced from local farms. This focus on purity and sustainability sets them apart from larger, mass-produced brands that may use synthetic ingredients.

Once you've identified your USP, it should be woven into your brand message and communicated consistently across all marketing materials.

Ensuring Consistent Messaging Across All Channels

Consistency is key when it comes to building a strong brand. Your audience should have a cohesive experience with your brand, whether they're visiting your website, following you on social media, or receiving an email from you.

Here's how to ensure consistency in your messaging:

1. **Create Brand Guidelines**: Develop a brand style guide that outlines your tone of voice, key messages, and visual elements (like fonts, colors, and logo usage). This will ensure that everyone on your team is aligned and that your brand is presented consistently across all platforms.
2. **Tailor Your Message to the Platform**: While your core message should stay the same, you may need to adjust the way you present it depending on the platform. For example, your Instagram posts might focus more on visual storytelling, while your blog posts dive deeper into educational content. However, the overall message and brand

values should remain consistent.
3. **Stay True to Your Values**: Consistency isn't just about the words you use—it's about staying true to your brand's values and mission. If sustainability is at the core of your brand, for instance, make sure that every message you send aligns with that value. Your actions should match your words.

Case Study: Consistency in Branding

Let's look at a successful local coffee shop that has built a loyal following through consistent branding. Their USP is that they offer ethically sourced coffee beans and support local farmers. They weave this message into everything they do:

- Their social media posts share stories about the farmers who grow their beans, highlighting their commitment to ethical sourcing.
- Their website features educational blog posts about the importance of sustainability in the coffee industry.
- Even their in-store experience reflects their brand values, with compostable cups and a discount for customers who bring reusable mugs.

By staying consistent in their messaging across all channels, they've built a strong, recognizable brand that resonates with their values-driven audience.

Action Steps for Crafting Your Organic Marketing Strategy

Now that you understand the components of an organic marketing strategy, let's recap with some actionable steps to help you get started:

1. **Set SMART Goals**: Define clear, actionable goals using the SMART framework. These goals should align with your overall business objectives.
2. **Create Customer Personas**: Spend time getting to know your audience. Create detailed personas that include demographics, psychographics, pain points, and buying behaviors.
3. **Define Your USP**: What makes your business unique? Identify your unique selling proposition and make sure it's clear in all of your marketing materials.
4. **Develop Consistent Messaging**: Create brand guidelines that outline your tone, messaging, and visual identity. Ensure that your message is consistent across all channels, from social media to email marketing to your website.
5. **Regularly Review and Adjust**: Your strategy should be flexible. As your business grows, or as you learn more about your audience, don't be afraid to adjust your approach.

Remember, creating a successful organic marketing strategy isn't about doing everything at once. It's about starting with clear goals, knowing your audience, and building a consistent, authentic brand that resonates with the people you want to serve.

By following these steps and keeping your strategy aligned with your broader business objectives, you'll be well on your way to building a strong, sustainable marketing foundation that supports long-term growth.

CHAPTER 3: DEVELOPING AN EFFECTIVE CONTENT STRATEGY

Welcome to one of the most exciting and essential parts of your organic marketing journey: **content**. If you've heard the phrase "content is king" and wondered why, you're in the right place. For small businesses, content is more than just words on a page—it's your secret weapon to building a brand that attracts, engages, and builds trust with your audience without the need for a massive marketing budget.

In this chapter, we'll dive into why content is key to organic marketing success, explore the different types of content you can create, and show you how to tell your brand's story in a way that resonates with your audience. Whether you're a content newbie or you've been writing blogs for years, you'll find actionable steps and insights that will elevate your content game and help your business grow.

Why Content is Key to Organic Marketing Success

Let's start with the basics: why is content so important? In the simplest terms, content is how your business **communicates with the world**. It's how potential customers find you, how they get to know what you stand for, and ultimately, how they decide whether or not to trust you enough to make a purchase.

Unlike paid marketing, where you spend money to grab attention, **organic content** works for you over time, delivering value to your audience long after it's been created. A blog post written today could bring in customers for years to come. A single YouTube video could attract thousands of views, building your audience with every play.

Content Drives Traffic

Every piece of content you create is an opportunity to **drive traffic** to your website or social media platforms. Let's say you own a local coffee shop and write a blog post titled, "5 Ways to Brew the Perfect Cup of Coffee at Home." That post, optimized with the right keywords, could show up in search results when someone Googles "how to brew coffee." Suddenly, they've discovered your coffee shop, and if they like what they see, they may sign up for your newsletter, follow you on Instagram, or even stop by for a latte.

Unlike paid ads, which stop driving traffic once your budget runs out, content continues to bring in traffic organically. This is what makes content marketing so powerful: it's **evergreen**. High-quality content builds a foundation for long-term success, making it one of the best investments you can make in your marketing strategy.

Content Engages Your Audience

Content isn't just about getting people to visit your website—it's also about **keeping them engaged**. The internet is flooded with information, so it's important that your content not only attracts attention but also holds it. Engaging content keeps people on your website longer, encourages them to follow you on social media, and builds a relationship with your brand.

Consider a fitness studio that regularly posts workout tips and motivational content on Instagram. By providing value and engaging with followers through comments, likes, and direct messages, they've created a community of people who feel connected to the brand. This engagement is key to turning casual followers into loyal customers.

Content Builds Trust

Trust is the currency of organic marketing, and content is one of the most effective ways to **build that trust**. When potential customers find your blog post, video, or podcast, they get to know your brand without feeling like they're being sold to. Instead, they're learning something, getting inspired, or finding solutions to their problems—all while associating your business with value and expertise.

The more value you provide through your content, the more people will come to trust your brand. And when people trust you, they're far more likely to buy from you, recommend you to others, and become loyal customers. Whether you're offering advice, sharing a behind-the-scenes look at your business, or telling stories about how you've helped other customers, each piece of content adds a **building block** to that trust.

Types of Content for Small Businesses

Now that you understand the importance of content in organic marketing, let's talk about the different types of content you can create. One of the great things about content marketing is that there are so many formats to choose from, so you can pick the ones that best fit your business and audience.

Here's a look at some of the most effective content types for small businesses:

1. Blogs

Blogging is one of the most **cost-effective** ways to drive traffic and engage your audience. A blog allows you to dive deep into topics relevant to your industry and provide value to your readers. It's also great for improving your SEO (Search Engine Optimization), helping your business rank higher in search engine results.

For example, if you run a pet grooming business, you could write blog posts on topics like "How to Keep Your Dog's Coat Healthy Between Grooming Sessions" or "5 Tips for Grooming a Nervous Cat." Each post is an opportunity to share your expertise and answer questions your customers are already asking.

Blogging also provides a way for you to **showcase your personality** and give your audience a sense of who you are as a brand. A bakery could write a blog post about the inspiration behind their newest cake recipe or share the story of how they started their business. This storytelling helps humanize your brand and makes customers feel more connected to you.

2. Infographics

Infographics are perfect for distilling complex information into a **visually appealing**, easy-to-digest format. People love visuals, and infographics make it easy to share valuable information in a way that's engaging and shareable.

For example, a financial advisor could create an infographic titled "The 5 Key Steps to Financial Freedom" that breaks down key concepts like saving, investing, and debt management into simple, bite-sized tips. This kind of content is great for sharing on social media, and it's highly **shareable**, which means your audience may spread it to their own networks, increasing your reach.

3. Case Studies

Case studies are incredibly effective because they show potential customers **real-world examples** of how your product or service has helped someone else. It's one thing to say, "We can solve your problem." It's another to provide detailed, step-by-step proof of how you did just that for a past customer.

For example, if you're a digital marketing consultant, you could write a case study showing how you helped a local restaurant increase their online reservations by 50% in three months. Include specific metrics and details to make the story compelling and credible. This not only builds trust but also gives potential customers a clear idea of what they can expect from working with you.

4. Videos

Video content is one of the most engaging formats available. People are increasingly consuming video on platforms like YouTube, Instagram, and TikTok, and it's a great way to **showcase your brand's personality** in a more dynamic way than text or images.

If you're a fitness coach, for example, you might create a series of short workout videos that your followers can do at home. If you're a clothing boutique, you could post "behind the scenes" videos showing how you curate your collections or how a particular product is made. Videos don't have to be highly produced to be effective—they just need to be authentic and provide value.

5. Podcasts

Podcasts are becoming a popular way for businesses to connect with their audience, especially if your target audience is busy and prefers to consume content on the go. With a podcast, you can share your expertise, interview industry experts, or dive into in-depth discussions that offer real value to your listeners.

For example, if you're a small business consultant, you could start a podcast where you share tips for business growth, interview successful entrepreneurs, or discuss industry trends. Podcasts build a deeper connection with your audience because they can hear your voice and feel like they're having a conversation with you, which helps build **trust and loyalty**.

The Power of Storytelling in Content Creation

No matter which type of content you choose to create, one element should always be present: **storytelling**. People are wired to connect with stories. Stories evoke emotion, create connections, and make your content more memorable. If you want your audience to engage with your content and remember your brand, storytelling is the key.

Why Storytelling Works

Think about the brands you love. Chances are, they've told you a story—whether it's their brand's origin, the story of their founder, or stories from real customers who have benefited from their product or service. These stories are what make you feel connected to the brand.

Your brand has a story, too, and sharing that story can help humanize your business. It could be a story about why you started your business, the challenges you've overcome, or even a customer success story that showcases the impact of your product or service.

Let's look at an example: A local flower shop could tell the story of how they source their flowers from a family-owned farm nearby, highlighting the personal connection between the farm and the shop. By weaving in stories about the family who runs the farm, how they take care of their flowers, and why it's important to support local agriculture, the flower shop creates an emotional connection with their audience. Suddenly, buying flowers isn't just a transaction—it's supporting a meaningful story.

How to Use Storytelling in Your Content

Here are a few ways to incorporate storytelling into your content strategy:

1. **Share Your Why**: Why did you start your business? What's your mission? Sharing your "why" helps customers understand your values and connect with your brand on a deeper level. For example, if you run a sustainable clothing brand, tell the story of why you're passionate about eco-friendly fashion and how your products contribute to a better planet.
2. **Tell Customer Success Stories**: Customer success stories or testimonials are powerful forms of storytelling. When a customer shares how your product or service has helped them, it not only builds trust but also shows other potential customers that you can solve their problems, too.
3. **Document Your Journey**: Share behind-the-scenes stories about your business, whether it's about product development, a day in the life of your team, or the challenges you've faced as a small business owner. These personal stories make your brand more relatable and give your audience a glimpse of the humans behind the brand.

Actionable Storytelling Tip: The Hero's Journey

One of the most effective storytelling frameworks is the **Hero's Journey**, a narrative structure that has been used in everything from ancient myths to blockbuster movies. In marketing, your customer is the hero, and your brand is the guide that helps them overcome their challenges and reach their goals.

Here's how it works:

- **Step 1**: The customer (hero) faces a challenge or problem.

- **Step 2**: They search for a solution, and that's where your product or service comes in.
- **Step 3**: With your help, they overcome the problem and achieve their desired outcome.

By positioning your customer as the hero of the story, you make your content more **relatable** and **engaging**. Your audience should see themselves in the story and feel like you understand their struggles—and, more importantly, that you have the solution.

Content Creation Tips

Now that we've covered the importance of content and the types you can create, let's focus on how to make that content **value-driven**, **shareable**, and **engaging**. It's one thing to produce content—it's another to make it resonate with your audience and inspire action. In this section, we'll discuss practical tips for creating content that doesn't just sit on your blog or social media feed but actually drives interaction, shares, and conversions.

How to Create Value-Driven, Shareable, and Engaging Content

1. **Start with Your Audience's Needs**

To create content that's valuable, you need to know what your audience wants. What problems are they facing? What questions do they have? What are their interests and pain points? By focusing on the needs of your audience, you can create content that provides **solutions** and offers real value.

For example, if you run a small gardening business, you could create a series of blog posts or videos on topics like "How to Start a Vegetable Garden for Beginners" or "The Best Plants for Small Spaces." These pieces of content directly address the interests and needs of your audience, providing them with useful information they can act on.

Actionable Tip: Create content that answers the most common questions your customers ask. Use surveys, social media polls, or customer feedback to gather insights into what topics will provide the most value.

2. Focus on Storytelling and Emotion

Content that tells a story and taps into emotion is far more likely to be shared. People are naturally drawn to stories that resonate with them—whether it's an inspiring success story, a funny anecdote, or a heartfelt personal journey.

For instance, if you run a local restaurant, you could create a video telling the story of how your business started. Or, you could share stories about the local farmers who provide your fresh ingredients. This type of content humanizes your brand and makes your audience feel more connected to you on a personal level.

Actionable Tip: Use customer testimonials and success stories as part of your content strategy. Let your audience see the real-world impact of your products or services.

3. Make It Interactive

Interactive content encourages your audience to **participate**. This can be anything from a poll or quiz to a simple call to action asking them to comment, share, or tag a friend. The more you can involve your audience in the conversation, the more engaged they'll be.

For example, a fitness studio could post a poll asking followers to vote on which type of workout they'd like to see next. Or, a fashion boutique might create an Instagram Story quiz where followers guess the latest style trends. Not only does this boost engagement, but it also gives you direct feedback from your audience, helping you tailor future content to their preferences.

4. **Include a Clear Call to Action (CTA)**

Whether you want your audience to share your content, sign up for your newsletter, or make a purchase, it's important to include a **clear call to action**. A CTA guides your audience toward the next step, making it easy for them to take action.

For example, at the end of a blog post, you could say, "If you found this guide helpful, share it with a friend or subscribe to our newsletter for more tips!" On social media, you might use CTAs like "Double-tap if you agree" or "Tag someone who needs to hear this."

Repurposing Content for Different Platforms

One of the smartest ways to make the most of your content is by **repurposing** it for different platforms. This means taking one piece of content and adapting it for various formats, ensuring that you reach a broader audience without constantly having to create new material.

Here's how you can repurpose content effectively:

- **Turn a Blog Post into Multiple Social Media Posts**: If you've written a long-form blog post, break it down into smaller snippets to share on social media. For example, if you wrote "10 Tips for Growing Your Own Herbs," you could create 10 individual posts, each highlighting one tip.
- **Transform a Video into a Blog Post**: If you've created a video tutorial, turn it into a written blog post by transcribing the key points. This allows you to reach both visual learners and readers who prefer written content.
- **Create Infographics from Data-Heavy Content**: If you've written a case study or research-heavy blog post, repurpose the key data points into an infographic. This makes the information easier to digest and share,

particularly on platforms like Pinterest and Instagram.
- **Use Podcast Quotes as Social Media Graphics**: If you run a podcast, pull key quotes or insights from each episode and turn them into visually appealing social media posts. This not only repurposes the content but also promotes the podcast to your audience.

Actionable Tip: When creating content, always think about how you can extend its lifespan by adapting it for different platforms. This saves you time and effort while ensuring you're consistently providing value across all your channels.

Content Planning and Scheduling

Creating high-quality content is important, but to really succeed with organic marketing, you need a plan. A **content calendar** helps you stay organized, ensures consistency, and allows you to plan your content around key events, product launches, or seasonal trends. It's the backbone of a strategic content marketing plan.

Developing a Content Calendar

A content calendar is a schedule that outlines what content you will publish, when, and where. It helps you plan ahead, stay consistent, and ensure that you're providing a mix of content types across different platforms.

Here's how to develop a simple, effective content calendar:

1. **Set Clear Goals**: Start by defining your content goals. Are you trying to increase website traffic? Grow your social media following? Generate more leads? Your goals will influence what kind of content you create and how often you publish.
2. **Choose Your Platforms**: Decide where you're going to focus your content efforts. Are you publishing blog

posts twice a week? Posting on Instagram daily? Hosting a weekly podcast? Your calendar should reflect all of the platforms where you plan to share content.

3. **Create a Posting Schedule**: Consistency is key in content marketing. Create a schedule that outlines when you'll publish each piece of content. For example, you might decide to post a new blog every Monday, share an infographic on Instagram on Wednesdays, and send out an email newsletter every Friday.
4. **Mix It Up**: Make sure your content calendar includes a variety of content types to keep your audience engaged. For example, one week you might post a customer testimonial video, and the next week, you might share a how-to blog post.
5. **Plan Around Key Dates**: Consider planning your content around relevant holidays, industry events, or product launches. For example, a fitness coach could plan a series of posts leading up to the New Year, offering tips for setting fitness resolutions.

Actionable Tip: Start by creating a simple calendar using tools like Google Sheets or Excel, and gradually expand it as you develop more content.

Tools for Managing and Scheduling Content

There are several tools available that can help you manage, schedule, and automate your content, ensuring that it goes out on time and reaches your audience consistently. Here are a few of the most popular tools:

- **Buffer**: Buffer is a simple, user-friendly tool that lets you schedule social media posts in advance across multiple platforms. You can plan and track your posts, see how they're performing, and adjust your strategy based on real-time insights.
- **Hootsuite**: Hootsuite offers more advanced features,

- including content scheduling, social listening, and analytics. It's a great tool for businesses that manage multiple social media accounts and want a centralized dashboard to monitor everything.
- **Later**: This tool is particularly popular for Instagram and Pinterest scheduling, allowing you to visually plan out your posts and ensure they fit with your overall aesthetic.
- **Trello**: Trello isn't a content scheduling tool, but it's perfect for managing the content creation process. You can create boards for each piece of content, assign tasks to your team, and track progress, ensuring that everything stays on schedule.
- **CoSchedule**: This tool combines content scheduling with project management. It allows you to plan your entire content strategy, from blog posts to social media updates, in one easy-to-use calendar.

Actionable Tip: Experiment with different scheduling tools to find the one that best fits your workflow. The goal is to simplify your content planning process and ensure that your content goes out consistently.

Mastering Content for Organic Growth

Content truly is king when it comes to organic marketing, but it's not just about creating random posts or articles. It's about **strategic, value-driven content** that connects with your audience, builds trust, and drives long-term growth.

By understanding the role of content in your marketing strategy, selecting the right formats, and incorporating storytelling, you can create content that not only engages your audience but also helps your business thrive. Whether you're repurposing content across platforms or using a content calendar to stay consistent, the key is to focus on quality and authenticity.

Remember, the most successful content marketing strategies are those that **put the audience first**, providing them with value, solutions, and inspiration. So, start planning, get creative, and let your content work its magic as you build your brand organically.

CHAPTER 4: MASTERING SOCIAL MEDIA FOR ORGANIC GROWTH

Welcome to the powerhouse of organic marketing: **social media**. In today's world, mastering social media is essential for small business owners who want to grow organically and connect with their audience. With billions of active users across platforms like Facebook, Instagram, LinkedIn, Twitter, TikTok, and Pinterest, social media offers an incredible opportunity to reach new customers, build relationships, and elevate your brand—all without spending a dime on ads.

In this chapter, we're going to break down how to choose the right platforms, craft engaging content that sparks conversations, and leverage social proof to build trust. You'll learn actionable strategies that help you create real, authentic growth on social media, without relying on paid campaigns.

Choosing the Right Social Media Platforms

One of the first questions that every small business owner faces is: **which social media platforms should I use?** With so many options available, it's easy to feel overwhelmed. Should you be on Facebook, Instagram, LinkedIn, TikTok, Pinterest, or Twitter? The key is not to be on every platform, but to be on the **right platforms** for your business and your audience.

Each social media platform has its own strengths, style, and user base. Your goal is to figure out where your target audience spends most of their time and what type of content works best for your business. Let's start by understanding the strengths of each platform.

Understanding the Strengths of Each Platform

1. Facebook: Community and Versatility

With over 2.8 billion monthly active users, Facebook remains one of the largest and most versatile platforms. It's a great place to **build a community**, especially through Facebook Groups, and allows you to share a variety of content types, including long-form posts, photos, videos, and links.

For small businesses, Facebook is especially powerful for:

- **Building a loyal community**: Facebook Groups allow you to foster deeper connections with your audience by creating a space for discussions, sharing, and engagement.
- **Promoting events**: If you're hosting events (either in person or online), Facebook's event feature makes it easy to promote and invite people directly.
- **Appealing to an older demographic**: While Instagram and TikTok are more popular with younger audiences, Facebook tends to have a broader age range, especially with users over 35.

Example: A local gym could create a Facebook Group for members where they can share fitness tips, success stories, and ask questions. This creates a sense of community and encourages more interaction outside of the gym.

2. Instagram: Visual Storytelling

Instagram is a visual-first platform that's perfect for businesses that rely on strong visuals, like retail, fashion, food, and travel. It's great for **showcasing products**, sharing behind-the-scenes moments, and building a brand's personality through Stories, Reels, and IGTV.

Instagram is ideal for:

- **Visual content**: Beautiful images and videos shine on Instagram, making it a perfect fit for businesses that can showcase their products or services visually.
- **Telling your brand's story**: Instagram Stories and Reels are fantastic tools for sharing behind-the-scenes content, day-in-the-life posts, or more casual, raw moments that make your brand relatable.
- **Engaging younger audiences**: Instagram skews younger, with a large user base among millennials and Gen Z.

Example: A handmade jewelry brand could use Instagram to share visually stunning images of their products, showcase the jewelry-making process in Reels, and post customer photos of them wearing the pieces in Stories to build trust and excitement.

3. LinkedIn: Professional Networking and B2B Growth

LinkedIn is the go-to platform for **B2B** (business-to-business) companies, professional networking, and thought leadership. It's ideal for service-based businesses, consultants, and industries that want to connect with other professionals or corporate clients.

Key strengths of LinkedIn include:

- **Building authority**: LinkedIn is a great place to publish articles, share industry insights, and position yourself as an expert in your field.

- **Professional networking**: If you're trying to connect with decision-makers or industry leaders, LinkedIn allows you to reach them directly.
- **B2B sales and marketing**: LinkedIn is particularly useful for generating leads and building relationships with other businesses.

Example: A marketing consultant could regularly publish articles on LinkedIn about digital marketing trends, participate in conversations with industry leaders, and use the platform to connect with potential clients.

4. Twitter: Real-Time Conversations and Industry Trends

Twitter is a fast-paced platform known for its real-time nature. It's perfect for staying on top of trends, engaging in industry discussions, and offering quick updates.

Twitter works well for:

- **Joining conversations**: Twitter is all about interacting in real-time. You can jump into trending conversations, comment on industry news, or respond to customer queries quickly.
- **Customer service**: Many companies use Twitter as a customer service channel to quickly respond to questions and concerns.
- **Sharing bite-sized content**: Twitter's 280-character limit forces you to be concise, making it ideal for sharing quick tips, news, or insights.

Example: A small tech company could use Twitter to share updates about their latest products, respond to customer inquiries, and participate in trending tech conversations.

5. TikTok: Creativity and Viral Content

TikTok is all about **short-form video content** that's creative, fun, and often humorous. It's one of the fastest-growing platforms, with a strong base among Gen Z and millennials.

TikTok excels at:

- **Creating viral content**: TikTok's algorithm can make even small accounts go viral, as long as the content is engaging and creative.
- **Connecting with a younger audience**: If your target market includes Gen Z or younger millennials, TikTok is the place to be.
- **Sharing quick tips or tutorials**: The platform's short video format is perfect for demonstrating how to use your products or providing value in quick, bite-sized pieces.

Example: A makeup artist could use TikTok to share quick makeup tutorials, participate in trending challenges, or give product recommendations in an entertaining way.

6. Pinterest: Visual Discovery and Shopping Inspiration

Pinterest is often seen as a **visual search engine**, making it great for businesses in industries like home decor, fashion, DIY, and food. Users come to Pinterest for inspiration and often use the platform to plan purchases.

Pinterest is best for:

- **Driving traffic**: Pinterest is fantastic for driving traffic to your website, blog, or eCommerce store. Users who save your pins are likely to revisit them later and take action.
- **Reaching customers in "planning mode"**: Pinterest users often browse with a specific goal in mind, like planning a wedding, redecorating a home, or searching for DIY projects.
- **Evergreen content**: Pins have a longer shelf life compared to posts on other platforms, meaning they can continue driving traffic and engagement long after

they're posted.

Example: A wedding planner could use Pinterest to share wedding inspiration boards, showcase real weddings they've planned, and drive traffic to their website through detailed blog posts.

Identifying Which Platforms Best Suit Your Business and Audience

Now that you have a sense of the strengths of each platform, the next step is identifying which ones are the best fit for your business and audience. You don't need to be on every platform—just the ones that align with your business goals and where your audience is most active.

Here's a step-by-step approach to choosing the right platforms:

1. **Know Your Audience**: The first question to ask yourself is, **Where is my audience?** If your target audience consists of professionals or B2B clients, LinkedIn might be your best bet. If you're targeting young, creative individuals, TikTok or Instagram might be a better fit.
2. **Consider Your Content**: What type of content do you enjoy creating, and what resonates with your brand? If your business is highly visual (fashion, food, design), Instagram or Pinterest will likely serve you well. If you're focused on thought leadership or professional services, LinkedIn or Twitter might be more suitable.
3. **Assess Your Resources**: Managing multiple platforms can be time-consuming. If you're a small business owner with limited resources, it's better to focus on **one or two platforms** and do them well rather than spreading yourself too thin across several platforms.
4. **Experiment and Adapt**: If you're not sure which platform is right for you, start by experimenting with one

or two and see how your audience responds. You can always adjust your strategy based on what works best.

Actionable Tip: Use analytics tools on each platform to monitor engagement, follower growth, and content performance. These insights will help you identify which platforms are generating the most results and where you should focus your efforts.

Creating Engaging Social Media Content

Once you've identified the right platforms, the next challenge is **creating content** that engages your audience. The key to social media success is producing content that sparks conversations, encourages interaction, and ultimately leads to deeper connections with your followers.

How to Design Posts That Spark Conversations and Encourage Interaction

Social media isn't just about broadcasting your message—it's about **starting conversations**. When your content sparks engagement, it increases visibility, builds relationships, and helps turn casual followers into loyal customers. Here's how to design posts that encourage interaction:

1. **Ask Questions**: One of the simplest ways to boost engagement is to ask your audience questions. People love sharing their opinions, so questions like, "What's your favorite product in our new collection?" or "How do you take your coffee?" can be incredibly effective. Questions make your audience feel involved and encourage them to comment on your posts.
2. **Use Polls and Quizzes**: Interactive content like polls and quizzes invites your audience to participate in a fun and engaging way. For example, an interior designer could run an Instagram Story poll asking fol-

lowers to choose between two different room designs.
3. **Encourage User-Generated Content (UGC)**: User-generated content is a powerful way to build trust and community. Encourage your followers to share their experiences with your product or service and feature their content on your page. This not only shows that people love your brand but also gives your audience a voice.
4. **Tell Stories**: People connect with stories on an emotional level. Share behind-the-scenes content, personal stories, or customer success stories to make your posts more relatable and engaging. For example, a restaurant could share the story of how a new dish was created, or a fitness trainer could post a client's transformation journey.
5. **Use Visuals and Video**: Posts with images and videos get significantly more engagement than text-only posts. Use high-quality visuals, behind-the-scenes photos, and videos to capture attention and encourage shares. Even short, authentic videos (think Instagram Reels or TikTok) can generate huge engagement.

Case Study: Starbucks' Use of Interactive Content

Starbucks is a master at using interactive content to engage its audience. The company often posts polls, questions, and user-generated content on Instagram and Twitter, asking followers to share their favorite drinks, vote on new flavors, or participate in seasonal promotions. By making their audience feel involved in the brand, Starbucks creates a loyal, engaged following.

Using User-Generated Content and Social Proof

User-generated content (UGC) is one of the most effective ways to build trust and showcase your product or service in a real-world context. When customers share photos, videos, or reviews about your business, it acts as **social proof**, showing others that real people use and love what you offer.

Here's how to incorporate UGC and social proof into your social media strategy:

1. **Encourage Your Audience to Share**: Make it easy for your customers to share their experiences. You can run campaigns asking them to post photos or reviews using a specific hashtag, or offer incentives like discounts or giveaways in exchange for sharing.
2. **Feature Customer Stories**: Highlighting customer stories or testimonials builds trust with your audience. Share their posts, tag them in your content, and create posts that showcase their experiences. For example, a clothing brand could feature photos of customers wearing their outfits with captions that highlight the customer's story.
3. **Leverage Reviews and Testimonials**: If your customers leave glowing reviews on Yelp, Google, or your website, don't let those stay hidden! Share them on social media. This reinforces the message that real people love your business and adds credibility.
4. **Create UGC Challenges**: A fun way to generate more user content is by running a UGC challenge. For example, a fitness brand could create a 30-day workout challenge, encouraging customers to post daily photos or videos of their progress using a branded hashtag.

Actionable Tip: Always ask for permission before sharing UGC, and give credit to the original creator by tagging them in your post. This not only shows appreciation but also fosters stronger relationships with your customers.

Mastering social media for organic growth begins with choosing the right platforms and creating content that truly engages your audience. By focusing on the strengths of each platform and designing posts that spark conversations, you'll build a community of loyal followers who feel connected to your brand. Incorporating user-generated content and social proof will further enhance trust and credibility, turning your social media presence into a powerful tool for organic business growth.

Mastering Social Media for Organic Growth

In the first part of this chapter, we explored how to choose the right social media platforms and create content that sparks conversations and builds engagement. Now, it's time to go deeper into what truly makes social media a powerful tool for **organic business growth**: **building a community** and **working with social media algorithms** to maximize your organic reach.

Growing a loyal and engaged community isn't about quick wins or viral posts; it's about fostering meaningful, authentic relationships. It's about creating a space where your audience feels heard, valued, and connected to your brand. And when you understand how to work with the algorithms that power each social platform, you'll be able to extend your reach even further, ensuring your content is seen by the right people at the right time.

Building a Community

Social media isn't just about getting followers—it's about **building a community**. A community is more than just people who follow your page; it's a group of engaged individuals who interact with your content, share your values, and advocate for your brand. A strong community can become the backbone of your business, fueling growth through word-of-mouth marketing, repeat business, and customer loyalty.

Engaging with Followers Through Comments, Shares, and Dir-

ect Messages

Engagement is the foundation of community building. The more you interact with your audience, the more they feel connected to you and your brand. Here's how you can actively engage with your followers across different platforms:

1. Reply to Comments

When someone takes the time to leave a comment on your post, whether it's a question, compliment, or suggestion, make sure to **respond**. This simple act shows your audience that you're listening and that you care about their input. It also encourages others to engage because they know they'll receive a response.

For example, a small café might post a picture of a new pastry and receive comments like, "This looks delicious!" A great way to respond would be, "Thank you! We'd love to hear what you think if you stop by to try it!" This not only keeps the conversation going but also subtly invites the follower to visit the café.

2. Start Conversations

Don't wait for followers to engage with you—take the initiative. Ask questions in your captions, encourage feedback, and prompt your audience to share their thoughts. For instance, a fashion boutique could post two photos of new outfits and ask, "Which look would you wear on a night out? Let us know in the comments!" By inviting people to participate, you create a dialogue that builds community.

3. Use Direct Messages (DMs) to Build Personal Connections

Direct messages offer a more **personal way** to engage with your audience. If someone sends you a message asking for advice or a recommendation, take the time to respond thoughtfully. DMs can also be used to follow up with customers who've had a great experience with your brand, turning one-time buyers into loyal fans.

For example, a fitness coach could DM someone who's expressed interest in their services and offer a personalized tip or suggestion based on the person's fitness goals. This one-on-one engagement shows that you care about their needs and helps build stronger relationships.

4. Encourage Shares and Mentions

Encourage your followers to share your content with their own networks by making it easy and fun for them to do so. For example, you could run a contest where followers share your post and tag friends for a chance to win a product or service. You can also prompt followers to mention your brand in their posts by using a branded hashtag or by asking them to share their experience with your product.

Example: A local restaurant might create a post asking customers to share photos of their meals and tag the restaurant for a chance to be featured on their page. This not only boosts engagement but also provides user-generated content that can be reshared to showcase happy customers.

Building Relationships Through Authentic Interaction

Social media is all about **authenticity**. In a world saturated with ads and impersonal messaging, people crave real, human connections. Your audience wants to know there's a person behind the brand, and the more authentic and genuine your interactions are, the more trust you'll build.

Here's how to create authentic interactions that help foster deeper relationships:

1. Be Transparent and Honest

Don't be afraid to show the real side of your business. Whether you're sharing behind-the-scenes moments, talking about the challenges you've faced, or being open about your values, authenticity builds trust. When your audience sees that you're not just a faceless business but a real person or team, they'll feel more connected to you.

For example, a skincare brand could share a post about the development process of their latest product, including any challenges or setbacks they encountered. This level of transparency shows honesty and builds credibility.

2. Celebrate Your Community

Show your followers that they're an essential part of your journey. Celebrate customer milestones, feature user-generated content, and acknowledge the support you receive from your community. This makes people feel valued and appreciated.

For instance, a yoga studio could regularly feature "Student Spotlights," where they highlight a community member's progress and share their story. This not only engages the individual but also encourages others in the community to participate.

3. Be Responsive and Accessible

Being responsive means not only replying to comments and DMs but also being **approachable**. Make it clear that your audience can reach out to you with questions, concerns, or feedback, and respond promptly when they do.

For example, a small eCommerce store could reply quickly to customer inquiries on Instagram, providing helpful responses and offering to resolve any issues right away. Being accessible builds trust and shows that you're dedicated to providing a great customer experience.

Social Media Algorithms and Organic Reach

If you've spent any time on social media, you've likely heard the word **"algorithm"** thrown around. Social media algorithms determine what content gets seen by users and how often it appears in their feeds. While the algorithms of platforms like Facebook, Instagram, and TikTok can sometimes feel mysterious, understanding how they work can help you maximize your organic reach and ensure your content gets seen by more people.

Understanding How Algorithms Work to Increase Organic Reach

Every social media platform uses an algorithm to prioritize which content users see first. These algorithms consider a variety of factors, including user behavior, engagement rates, and the relevance of the content. While each platform has its own unique algorithm, they generally aim to show users the content they're most likely to engage with.

Here are a few key factors that algorithms typically consider:

1. Engagement Rate

The more engagement (likes, comments, shares, and saves) your post gets, the more likely it is to be seen by a larger audience. Social media platforms reward engagement by boosting the visibility of posts that resonate with users. This means that the first few hours after you post are critical—if your followers engage with your content early on, the algorithm will push it out to more people.

2. Relevance

The algorithm prioritizes content that is relevant to users based on their past behavior. For example, if someone frequently interacts with posts about fitness, they're more likely to see content related to fitness in their feed. This is why it's important to consistently post content that aligns with your audience's interests and preferences.

3. Consistency

Social media platforms favor accounts that post consistently. If you're regularly posting high-quality content, the algorithm is more likely to prioritize your posts in the feed. On the other hand, sporadic posting can result in decreased visibility, as the algorithm won't see your account as active.

4. Time Spent on Content

The algorithm also looks at how long users spend interacting with your content. If someone watches your video to the end or spends a lot of time reading your post, this signals to the algorithm that your content is valuable and should be shown to more people.

Tips for Working with Platform Algorithms to Maximize Visibility

Now that you understand how algorithms work, let's talk about how you can **work with them** to increase your organic reach and ensure your content gets seen by more people.

1. Encourage Early Engagement

The first few hours after posting are crucial for determining how far your content will reach. To boost engagement early on, try the following strategies:

- **Post when your audience is most active**: Use analytics tools to determine when your followers are online and post during those times to increase the chances of immediate interaction.
- **Engage with your audience right after posting**: Respond to comments, ask follow-up questions, and like your followers' replies to encourage more conversation around your post.
- **Use strong calls-to-action (CTAs)**: Invite your audience to like, comment, or share your post with a compelling CTA. For example, a fitness trainer might post a

workout video and ask, "Which exercise is your favorite? Let me know in the comments!"

Example: A small bakery could post a new product launch at 9 AM, right when their local audience is active, and include a CTA like, "Comment below if you'd love to try this pastry today!" By encouraging early comments, the post is more likely to gain traction.

2. Consistently Post High-Quality Content

Consistency is key when it comes to staying visible in the social media algorithm. You don't need to post every day, but you do need to post **regularly**. Create a content schedule that you can realistically stick to, and prioritize quality over quantity.

- **Create a content calendar**: Plan out your posts ahead of time to ensure a steady stream of content. Consistent posting shows the algorithm that your account is active, increasing your chances of being featured in the feed.
- **Maintain quality**: Don't post just for the sake of posting. Make sure every piece of content you share provides value, whether that's through education, entertainment, or inspiration.

3. Use Platform-Specific Features

Every social media platform has unique features designed to engage users—whether it's Instagram Stories, TikTok challenges, or Facebook Live. Using these features can give your content an extra algorithmic boost.

- **Instagram Stories and Reels**: Instagram tends to prioritize accounts that use all of its features, especially Reels. Posting a Reel that resonates with your audience can lead to significant organic growth.
- **TikTok Trends**: TikTok's algorithm heavily favors trending content. If you can create a video that taps

into a trending song or challenge, you increase your chances of going viral.

Case Study: How a Small Boutique Used Reels for Growth

A local fashion boutique noticed that their Instagram feed posts weren't gaining as much traction as they'd hoped. After experimenting with Instagram Reels, they created short videos showcasing "How to Style [New Collection Item] for Fall," which started gaining far more engagement than their previous posts. The algorithm boosted their Reels, resulting in a 30% increase in followers in just a few weeks.

4. Focus on Engagement, Not Just Follower Count

The algorithm cares more about engagement than your follower count. An account with 1,000 highly engaged followers can outperform an account with 10,000 disengaged followers. Focus on building genuine connections and fostering real engagement, rather than simply growing your follower count.

- **Respond to every comment**: This encourages ongoing conversations and signals to the algorithm that your content is valuable.
- **Ask questions and prompt discussions**: Posts that encourage dialogue between users tend to perform better. For example, a coffee shop could post, "What's your go-to order in the morning? Let us know in the comments and tag a friend who's also a coffee lover!"

5. Experiment with Different Content Formats

Different formats (photos, videos, Stories, live streams) are treated differently by social media algorithms. Experiment with a mix of formats to see what resonates most with your audience and garners the highest engagement.

Actionable Tip: Review your analytics to see which formats perform best, then focus on creating more of that type of content. If video content consistently performs better than static images, for example, prioritize more video posts in your schedule.

Building a strong community and understanding how to work with social media algorithms are key to growing your business organically on social media. By actively engaging with your followers, creating authentic interactions, and leveraging the algorithm's signals, you can extend your reach and build a loyal, engaged audience that advocates for your brand.

Remember, success on social media is not about going viral overnight—it's about consistency, authenticity, and cultivating relationships over time. By focusing on building real connections with your community and understanding how algorithms prioritize content, you'll set your business up for sustainable, long-term growth. With the right strategies in place, your social media presence can become a powerful tool that drives organic success and amplifies your brand's impact.

CHAPTER 5: SEO—DRIVING ORGANIC TRAFFIC TO YOUR WEBSITE

In the vast ocean of online content, how do you make sure your small business stands out? The answer lies in **Search Engine Optimization (SEO)**. Whether you're running an eCommerce store, a local café, or a professional service, SEO is one of the most powerful tools you can leverage to grow your organic traffic without spending money on ads. When done right, SEO ensures that when potential customers search for products or services like yours, they find **you**—not your competitors.

In this chapter, we'll break down SEO in practical terms that any small business owner can understand and implement. From optimizing your website's content and structure (on-page SEO) to building your online authority with links and partnerships (off-page SEO), we'll cover everything you need to know to start driving more traffic to your website. And for those of you with a local customer base, we'll explore the importance of **local SEO**, so you can ensure you're the go-to business in your area.

Introduction to SEO: What is SEO, and Why It Matters for Small Businesses?

Search Engine Optimization (SEO) is the process of improving your website to increase its visibility when people search for products or services related to your business on search engines like Google. When someone types in a query—say, "best coffee shop in Austin"—Google sifts through billions of websites to present the most relevant and useful results.

If your website ranks highly on those search results, you have a better chance of attracting visitors who are actively looking for what you offer. **Ranking on the first page** is the goal because most people don't scroll past it. SEO helps you climb to those top spots by optimizing both the content on your website and your online reputation.

For small businesses, SEO offers several crucial benefits:

- **Cost-effective marketing**: Unlike paid ads, SEO continues to drive traffic long after you've implemented your strategy.
- **Trust and credibility**: Higher rankings are often perceived as more trustworthy, making people more likely to click through to your site.
- **Local visibility**: If you serve a specific geographic area, SEO can help you dominate local searches (more on this later).

Think of SEO as a marathon, not a sprint. It takes time, but the long-term benefits—more traffic, higher conversions, and greater brand awareness—make it a game-changing strategy for small businesses.

On-Page SEO: Optimizing Titles, Meta Descriptions, Headings, and Images

On-page SEO refers to the process of optimizing individual web pages to improve their rankings and earn more relevant traffic from search engines. It involves optimizing both the **content** and the **HTML source code** of a page.

Let's dive into the critical components of on-page SEO and how you can implement them for your website.

1. Optimizing Titles (Title Tags)

The title tag is one of the most important elements for on-page SEO. It tells both search engines and users what your page is about. It's the clickable headline that appears on the search engine results page (SERP).

Here's how to optimize your title tags:

- **Keep it under 60 characters**: Titles that are too long get cut off in search results. Keep it concise while clearly describing the content.
- **Include your target keyword**: Place your most important keyword close to the beginning of the title. This signals to search engines what your page is about.
- **Make it compelling**: A great title can entice people to click. Think about what will make someone choose your page over another. Use action words or promises, like "Discover," "Best," or "How to."

Example: Let's say you own a bakery and have a page about wedding cakes. Instead of just writing "Wedding Cakes," an optimized title might be: "Custom Wedding Cakes in Austin | Award-Winning Bakery."

2. Meta Descriptions

Meta descriptions are the short snippets of text that appear under your title tag in search results. While they don't directly affect your rankings, a well-crafted meta description can increase click-through rates by giving users a compelling reason to visit your site.

Here's how to optimize meta descriptions:

- **Stay within 155-160 characters**: Anything longer gets cut off in search results.
- **Include your target keyword**: Keywords in meta descriptions are bolded when they match the search query, making them stand out.
- **Incorporate a call-to-action (CTA)**: Encourage the user to take action, such as "Learn more," "Get started today," or "Explore our range of products."

Example: For a pet grooming service, a good meta description might be: "Looking for the best pet grooming in Chicago? Our experienced team offers top-quality care for dogs and cats. Book your appointment today!"

3. Headings (H1, H2, H3)

Headings organize your content, making it easier for both users and search engines to understand. The **H1** tag is the main heading of your page, while **H2**, **H3**, and other subheadings break up the content into sections.

Best practices for optimizing headings:

- **Use one H1 tag per page**: Your H1 tag should include your target keyword and give a clear idea of what the page is about.
- **Organize content with subheadings**: Use H2 and H3 tags to break your content into logical sections. This not only improves readability but also helps search engines better understand the structure of your content.
- **Include keywords in subheadings**: Naturally incorporate relevant keywords into your subheadings to reinforce the topic of the page.

4. Optimizing Images

Images enhance the user experience, but they can also help with SEO if optimized correctly.

Here's how to optimize images for SEO:

- **Use descriptive filenames**: Instead of uploading an image with a generic name like "IMG1234.jpg," use a descriptive name that includes your target keyword, such as "chocolate-wedding-cake.jpg."
- **Add alt text**: Alt text is used by screen readers to describe images to visually impaired users, but it's also a ranking factor. Include a concise description of the image with relevant keywords.
- **Compress image sizes**: Large images can slow down your site, which negatively impacts SEO. Use tools like TinyPNG to compress images without sacrificing quality.

Case Study: A Local Café's On-Page SEO Success

A local café in Seattle optimized their on-page SEO by focusing on titles, meta descriptions, and headings. They updated their homepage title to "Best Coffee in Seattle | Organic, Local, Handcrafted," added a meta description with a clear CTA, and organized their content with keyword-rich H2 tags like "Our Organic Coffee Menu" and "Seattle's Favorite Coffee Roasters." Within six months, their website's organic traffic increased by 40%, and they started appearing on the first page for searches like "best organic coffee Seattle."

Keywords: Research, Integration, and Avoiding Overstuffing

Keywords are the foundation of SEO. They're the words and phrases people type into search engines when looking for products or services like yours. Your goal is to identify the keywords your audience is searching for and integrate them naturally into your content.

1. Keyword Research

Keyword research is the process of finding the right keywords to target. There are many tools available to help you with this, such as Google Keyword Planner, Ubersuggest, and SEMrush.

Here's how to perform effective keyword research:

- **Start with broad topics**: Think about the main topics related to your business. For example, if you own a yoga studio, your broad topics might be "yoga classes," "meditation," and "yoga for beginners."
- **Find specific, long-tail keywords**: Long-tail keywords are longer, more specific phrases that usually have lower competition and are easier to rank for. For example, instead of targeting the highly competitive keyword "yoga," you might target "beginner yoga classes in Boston."
- **Analyze search volume and competition**: Look for keywords that have a decent search volume but aren't too competitive. This gives you the best chance of ranking on the first page.

2. Keyword Integration

Once you've identified your target keywords, it's time to integrate them into your content. But be careful—**keyword stuffing** (overloading your content with keywords) can hurt your rankings and make your content hard to read.

Here's how to integrate keywords naturally:

- **Use keywords in your title and headings**: Place your primary keyword in the title and main heading (H1), and include variations of the keyword in your subheadings (H2, H3).
- **Sprinkle keywords throughout the content**: Include your target keywords a few times in the body of your

content, but always prioritize readability and user experience. Use synonyms and related phrases to avoid repetition.
- **Don't forget your meta tags**: Include your target keywords in your meta description, title tags, and alt text for images.

Example: If you're a local accountant, a well-optimized blog post might be titled "Tax Tips for Small Businesses in Austin" with headings like "How to Save on Taxes" and "Best Accounting Practices for Entrepreneurs." The keywords "tax tips" and "small businesses" would appear naturally throughout the post.

Off-Page SEO: Building Backlinks and Improving Domain Authority

While on-page SEO focuses on optimizing your website's content, **off-page SEO** is about building your website's reputation and authority through **external factors** like backlinks.

1. Building Backlinks

Backlinks are links from other websites to your own. They act as a vote of confidence, signaling to search engines that your content is valuable and trustworthy. The more high-quality backlinks you have, the better your chances of ranking

higher in search results.

Here's how to build backlinks:

- **Create high-quality, shareable content**: The best way to attract backlinks is by creating content that people want to link to. This could be an in-depth blog post, an infographic, or a resource guide that provides real value to your audience.
- **Reach out to industry influencers**: Build relationships

with bloggers, influencers, and journalists in your industry. You can ask them to share or link to your content, but always offer something of value in return (such as a guest post or collaboration).
- **Write guest posts**: Guest blogging on reputable websites in your industry is a great way to build backlinks. It also helps you reach new audiences. Include a link back to your website in your author bio or within the content (when relevant).

Case Study: Guest Blogging for Backlinks

A small web design agency in New York wanted to improve their SEO rankings. They started writing guest posts for popular design blogs and included backlinks to their own website. Over six months, they wrote for ten different sites, earning high-quality backlinks each time. As a result, their domain authority improved, and they started ranking on the first page for competitive terms like "custom website design NYC."

2. Improving Domain Authority

Domain authority (DA) is a score developed by Moz that predicts how well a website will rank on search engines. It's based on factors like the number and quality of backlinks, site structure, and overall SEO performance. While you can't directly control your DA, improving your SEO practices can boost it over time.

Here's how to improve your domain authority:

- **Focus on getting high-quality backlinks**: Not all backlinks are created equal. A single link from a reputable site like Forbes or The New York Times is worth far more than multiple links from low-quality sites.
- **Create evergreen content**: Evergreen content is content that remains relevant over time. Creating in-depth guides, tutorials, and resources that people will want to link to for years is a great way to attract backlinks

consistently.
- **Stay up-to-date with SEO best practices**: SEO is always evolving. Keep an eye on Google's algorithm updates and adjust your strategy accordingly.

Local SEO for Small Businesses: Optimizing Your Google My Business Profile

If you have a brick-and-mortar store or serve a local customer base, **local SEO** is crucial. Local SEO focuses on optimizing your online presence to attract customers from specific geographic areas. When people search for "restaurants near me" or "plumbers in Los Angeles," local SEO ensures your business appears in the search results.

1. Optimizing Your Google My Business Profile

One of the most important aspects of local SEO is **Google My Business (GMB)**. GMB is a free tool that allows you to manage how your business appears in Google Search and Maps. By optimizing your GMB profile, you increase your chances of appearing in the **local pack**—the section of Google search results that shows local businesses relevant to the search query.

Here's how to optimize your Google My Business profile:

- **Complete all sections**: Make sure your profile is 100% complete, including your business name, address, phone number, website, business hours, and category.
- **Write a detailed business description**: Use your business description to explain what you offer, including relevant keywords that people might search for.
- **Add high-quality photos**: Businesses with photos on their GMB profile receive 42% more requests for directions and 35% more click-throughs to their website.
- **Encourage reviews**: Positive reviews are a major rank-

ing factor for local SEO. Encourage your happy customers to leave reviews on your Google My Business profile, and be sure to respond to both positive and negative reviews.

Case Study: A Local Plumber's Google My Business Optimization

A small plumbing company in Phoenix wanted to improve their local visibility. They optimized their Google My Business profile by adding high-quality photos, responding to every review, and keeping their business hours updated. Within three months, their business started showing up in the local pack for keywords like "emergency plumber in Phoenix," leading to a 25% increase in calls from local customers.

2. Local Citations and NAP Consistency

Local citations are mentions of your business's name, address, and phone number (NAP) on other websites, such as online directories, Yelp, and industry-specific platforms. Ensuring that your NAP information is consistent across all platforms is crucial for local SEO.

Here's how to build and optimize local citations:

- **Claim your listings**: Make sure your business is listed on major online directories like Yelp, Yellow Pages, and local chambers of commerce. Claim your business and ensure all information is correct.
- **Ensure NAP consistency**: Your business name, address, and phone number should be exactly the same across all online platforms. Inconsistent information can confuse search engines and hurt your rankings.

SEO is one of the most effective ways to drive long-term, sustainable traffic to your website. Whether you're optimizing your site's content (on-page SEO), building your online reputation through backlinks (off-page SEO), or focusing on dominating local searches, SEO is a powerful tool that can transform your small business's online presence.

By implementing the practical advice and actionable steps in this chapter, you'll be well on your way to improving your search rankings, attracting more organic traffic, and growing your business. Remember, SEO is a long-term strategy, so stay consistent, monitor your progress, and make adjustments as needed. The rewards —more visibility, credibility, and customers—are well worth the effort.

CHAPTER 6: EMAIL MARKETING— NURTURING RELATIONSHIPS ORGANICALLY

In a world saturated with social media and countless online ads, **email marketing** stands out as a powerful, reliable, and personal way to connect with your audience. For small business owners, email marketing offers an opportunity to build direct relationships with customers, nurture trust, and drive conversions—all while delivering one of the highest returns on investment (ROI) of any marketing channel.

You might wonder, with so many digital tools at our disposal, why is email marketing still relevant? The answer is simple: **it works**. Email gives you direct access to your audience's inbox, where you can engage with them on a more personal level than social media posts or website visitors. It's your chance to create tailored content that speaks directly to their interests, needs, and desires.

In this chapter, we'll explore the reasons why email marketing remains so effective, how to grow and nurture your email list, and how to craft campaigns that resonate with your audience. We'll also dive into **email automation**—an essential tool that will help you build relationships on autopilot.

Why Email Marketing is Still Effective

Despite the rise of social media, email remains one of the most effective and trusted communication tools for businesses. Here's why:

1. Direct, Personalized Relationships

Email allows you to speak to your audience one-on-one in a way that no other channel does. Social media platforms like Facebook and Instagram can be noisy, with your message easily lost among hundreds of other posts. But when someone opens your email, you've captured their undivided attention.

Personalization is one of the most powerful aspects of email marketing. By addressing your audience by name, sending tailored offers, or segmenting your list based on specific behaviors, you're able to create a personalized experience that resonates more deeply with each individual. Email gives you the opportunity to build trust over time, offering relevant content that keeps your subscribers engaged and coming back for more.

Example: A small fitness studio could send personalized emails to their clients based on the types of classes they've attended. For example, someone who regularly attends yoga could receive an email with exclusive discounts on yoga workshops, while those who prefer high-intensity training might receive tips on improving performance in their next class.

2. High ROI Compared to Other Channels

According to numerous studies, email marketing consistently delivers a **higher return on investment (ROI)** than almost any other marketing channel. In fact, for every $1 spent on email marketing, the average return is around **$36**. That's a powerful statistic, especially for small businesses looking to maximize their marketing budget.

Unlike paid ads, where the cost is ongoing and results may be fleeting, email marketing allows you to build relationships that last. Once someone joins your email list, they've given you permission to reach out to them again and again. Over time, as you provide value through your emails, those relationships can lead to repeat purchases, referrals, and increased brand loyalty.

Example: An online clothing boutique might spend $500 on an email marketing platform annually, but by sending out regular promotional campaigns, nurturing new subscribers, and offering exclusive discounts, they can generate thousands of dollars in repeat sales from their email list.

Building and Growing Your Email List

To get the most out of email marketing, you need to build a list of engaged subscribers who are interested in hearing from you. The key word here is **engaged**—you don't just want to collect emails for the sake of numbers. Your goal is to grow a list of people who genuinely want to receive your content and offers.

Techniques to Organically Grow Your Email Subscriber Base

1. **Offer Valuable Lead Magnets** One of the best ways to grow your email list is by offering something valuable in exchange for people's email addresses. These are called **lead magnets**—incentives that entice people to sign up for your list because they're getting something useful in return. Lead magnets can take many forms, depending on your industry and what would appeal most to your audience.
Here are some examples:
    - **eBooks**: A digital guide or eBook on a topic

relevant to your audience. For example, a real estate agent could offer a free guide on "10 Tips for First-Time Homebuyers."
- **Discount Codes**: Offering a discount code for first-time buyers can be a powerful way to entice people to sign up for your list. A local boutique might offer "10% off your first order" in exchange for an email sign-up.
- **Free Consultations**: Service-based businesses can offer a free initial consultation or audit. For instance, a marketing consultant might offer a 30-minute strategy session for anyone who joins their list.
- **Exclusive Content**: Some businesses offer subscribers exclusive content, such as early access to sales, behind-the-scenes looks, or special deals not available to the public.

2. **Use Opt-In Forms on Your Website** Placing **opt-in forms** strategically across your website can help you capture new subscribers organically. Make sure your forms are simple and easy to fill out. You can include opt-in forms in places like:
    - Your homepage
    - Blog posts
    - Pop-ups (with careful timing, such as after a visitor has spent some time on your site)
    - The footer of your website
    - Landing pages dedicated to specific offers (e.g., sign up for a free webinar)

3. **Example**: A bakery's website could have a pop-up offering a "Free Recipe Booklet with 10 Delicious Pastries" in exchange for an email sign-up. Visitors who join the list could receive this digital booklet directly in their inbox.

4. **Leverage Social Media** Social media can be an excellent tool for driving traffic to your email list sign-up page.

Use your platforms to promote your lead magnets, exclusive offers, or simply invite people to join your community for valuable content.

Actionable Tip: Run an Instagram campaign promoting a lead magnet, like "Sign up for our email list and get a free 7-day workout plan!" Include a link in your bio directing people to your sign-up page.

Using Lead Magnets to Grow Your List

Lead magnets are highly effective because they give potential subscribers an immediate benefit. If your lead magnet provides real value, people will be far more likely to share their email with you.

Here's how to create a lead magnet that works:

- **Solve a specific problem**: Your lead magnet should address a pain point or need that your audience has. The more relevant it is, the more likely they are to sign up.
- **Keep it simple**: Lead magnets don't have to be elaborate or time-consuming. A one-page checklist or guide can be just as effective as a 50-page eBook.
- **Use clear, compelling language**: In your opt-in form, clearly explain the value of your lead magnet. Use action words like "Get," "Download," or "Claim" to encourage people to take the next step.

Case Study: Growing a List with Lead Magnets A fitness trainer created a free "7-Day Home Workout Plan" as a lead magnet. By promoting it on her website and social media, she quickly grew her email list by 500 subscribers in just one month. Each new subscriber received the workout plan, followed by a series of emails introducing them to her paid programs. Over time, many of these subscribers became paying clients.

Crafting Effective Email Campaigns

Once you've built your list, the next step is creating email campaigns that **engage** your audience and keep them coming back for more. A well-crafted email can nurture relationships, provide value, and ultimately drive sales. But to succeed, you need more than just a generic message. You need to grab attention with compelling subject lines, provide useful content, and personalize the experience.

How to Create Engaging Subject Lines and Body Content

Your subject line is the first thing your subscribers will see when your email lands in their inbox. If it doesn't grab their attention, your email may never be opened. Here's how to craft subject lines that get noticed:

1. **Keep It Short and Sweet**: Aim for 6-10 words, so your subject line doesn't get cut off on mobile devices.
2. **Create Curiosity**: Give people a reason to open your email by sparking curiosity. For example, "The Secret to Perfect Coffee at Home" is more intriguing than "Our Coffee Products."
3. **Include Numbers or Lists**: People love lists because they're easy to digest. A subject line like "5 Easy Ways to Improve Your Fitness" is clear and actionable.
4. **Personalization**: Use your subscriber's first name in the subject line for a more personalized approach. For example, "Sarah, Here's Your Exclusive Offer" feels more personal than a generic subject line.

Once your email is opened, your **body content** needs to deliver on the promise of the subject line and keep your audience engaged. Here's how to do that:

1. **Write Like You're Talking to a Friend**: Keep your tone conversational and authentic. Write as if you're talking to a friend, not giving a corporate presentation.

2. **Provide Value**: Always lead with value. Whether it's helpful tips, exclusive offers, or industry insights, make sure your content serves your audience.
3. **Include a Clear Call to Action (CTA)**: Every email should have a specific goal. Do you want your subscribers to click a link, make a purchase, or read a blog post? Make your CTA clear and compelling.

Personalization and Segmentation for Improved Results

Personalization goes beyond just using someone's first name. It's about tailoring your emails to each subscriber's interests, behaviors, and preferences. The more personalized your emails are, the more likely your audience is to engage.

Email Automation: Setting Up Welcome Series, Nurture Campaigns, and Sales Follow-Ups

As a small business owner, your time is one of your most valuable resources. While crafting personalized emails for each individual customer might seem like an overwhelming task, **email automation** offers an elegant solution. With automation, you can set up a series of emails that are sent automatically based on a subscriber's actions, ensuring that each customer receives the right message at the right time without requiring constant manual effort.

In this section, we'll dive into the **power of email automation** and show you how to set up effective automated campaigns—such as welcome series, nurture campaigns, and sales follow-ups—that will help you build relationships, guide your customers through the buyer's journey, and ultimately increase conversions.

What is Email Automation?

Email automation refers to the process of setting up emails to be sent automatically based on specific triggers or behaviors. These triggers could include someone joining your email list, clicking a link in an email, making a purchase, or even abandoning their cart on your website.

Automation allows you to build **tailored sequences** that nurture relationships with your subscribers without having to manually send each email. This ensures that your audience consistently receives valuable, relevant content that moves them closer to becoming loyal customers.

The key benefits of email automation include:

- **Consistency**: With automation, you're able to stay in touch with your subscribers at key moments, even when you're busy running your business.
- **Personalization**: Automated emails can be highly personalized based on the actions a subscriber takes, making them feel like each email is tailored just for them.
- **Efficiency**: Automation saves you time by streamlining the process of sending out emails, allowing you to focus on other important aspects of your business.

Setting Up a Welcome Series

The **welcome series** is one of the most important automated email sequences you can set up. It's the first impression new subscribers have of your business, and it sets the tone for the rest of your relationship. A well-crafted welcome series builds trust, provides value, and invites subscribers to take the next step with your brand.

What is a Welcome Series?

A welcome series is a sequence of emails automatically sent to new subscribers after they join your list. These emails introduce them to your business, explain what they can expect, and guide them through their first interactions with your brand.

Here's what a typical welcome series might look like:

1. **Email 1: Welcome and Thank You**
     - **Objective**: Greet your new subscribers, thank them for joining your list, and give them an overview of what they can expect from your emails.
     - **Content**: Use a warm, welcoming tone and briefly introduce your business. Highlight the value your emails will provide (e.g., exclusive offers, tips, or behind-the-scenes content). If the subscriber signed up through a lead magnet, include a link to download or access it right away.
     - **Example CTA**: "Check out our most popular blog posts or follow us on social media for daily tips!"
2. **Email 2: Share Your Brand Story**
     - **Objective**: Build a personal connection by sharing the story behind your business, your mission, and why you do what you do.
     - **Content**: Tell the story of how your business started, what values drive your company, and how you aim to help your customers. Including personal anecdotes or challenges you've overcome can make this email more relatable.
     - **Example CTA**: "Reply to this email and let us know what you're most excited about—we'd love to hear from you!"
3. **Email 3: Highlight Your Products or Services**
     - **Objective**: Introduce your core offerings and explain how they solve your customers' problems or improve their lives.

- **Content**: Focus on the benefits of your products or services rather than just listing features. Include testimonials or success stories from happy customers to build trust.
- **Example CTA**: "Browse our best-selling products and find what's right for you."

4. **Email 4: Offer a Special Incentive**
   - **Objective**: Encourage your new subscribers to take action, such as making their first purchase or booking a consultation, by offering a special discount or bonus.
   - **Content**: Thank your subscribers for being part of your community and offer them a time-sensitive discount or free resource to motivate them to take the next step.
   - **Example CTA**: "Use code WELCOME10 at checkout for 10% off your first order—valid for the next 48 hours!"

Actionable Tip: Set up your welcome series using an email marketing platform like Mailchimp, ConvertKit, or ActiveCampaign. These platforms allow you to automate the sequence so that each email is sent at specific intervals (e.g., one day, three days, or a week after the previous email).

Nurture Campaigns: Building Relationships Over Time

Once your welcome series has introduced new subscribers to your brand, it's time to focus on nurturing those relationships over time. **Nurture campaigns** are designed to keep your audience engaged, provide ongoing value, and move them closer to making a purchase or taking other desired actions.

What is a Nurture Campaign?

A **nurture campaign** is a series of emails sent to subscribers over a longer period, with the goal of maintaining engagement, educating them about your offerings, and guiding them through the buyer's journey. These campaigns help you stay top-of-mind with your audience while building trust and credibility.

Nurture campaigns can include:

- **Educational content**: Provide tips, how-to guides, or insights that are relevant to your audience's interests or pain points.
- **Case studies or success stories**: Show how your products or services have helped real customers achieve their goals.
- **Product recommendations**: Based on a subscriber's previous behavior or interests, suggest products or services that might be a good fit for them.
- **Exclusive offers or updates**: Keep your audience informed about new products, promotions, or company news.

Example: A digital marketing agency might create a nurture campaign that includes:

1. A blog post about "The Top 5 Social Media Mistakes Businesses Make"
2. A case study showing how they helped a client increase online sales by 30%
3. A product recommendation email offering a free consultation for social media strategy

How to Craft an Effective Nurture Campaign

1. **Map Out the Customer Journey**: Think about the steps your audience takes before making a purchase. What questions do they have? What hesitations might they need to overcome? Your nurture campaign should ad-

dress these stages and provide content that moves them closer to a decision.
2. **Segment Your Audience**: If your subscribers have different interests or needs, consider creating separate nurture campaigns for each segment. For example, an online retailer might send one set of emails to subscribers who have shown interest in men's clothing and another set to those interested in women's accessories.
3. **Deliver Value Consistently**: Don't make every email in your nurture campaign about selling. Focus on providing real value, whether that's educational content, tips, or industry insights. The more helpful and relevant your emails are, the more likely your audience will engage with them over time.

Sales Follow-Up Campaigns: Turning Leads into Customers

Not everyone will make a purchase right away, and that's okay. Sometimes, a gentle reminder or additional information is all a potential customer needs to move forward. **Sales follow-up campaigns** are designed to re-engage leads and encourage them to take the final step toward conversion.

What is a Sales Follow-Up Campaign?

A **sales follow-up campaign** is an automated email sequence sent to subscribers who have shown interest in your products or services but haven't yet made a purchase. This could include people who added items to their cart but didn't check out, requested more information, or attended a webinar but didn't sign up for a service.

The goal of a sales follow-up campaign is to address any potential barriers to purchasing, provide additional motivation, and make it easy for the customer to complete the sale.

Setting Up a Sales Follow-Up Campaign

Here's an example of a simple sales follow-up campaign:

1. **Email 1: Gentle Reminder**
     - **Trigger**: Sent one day after a cart abandonment or inquiry.
     - **Objective**: Remind the customer of what they're missing out on and encourage them to complete the purchase.
     - **Content**: Use friendly language to remind the customer of the item(s) they left behind and offer a quick link to complete the checkout process.
     - **Example CTA**: "Looks like you left something in your cart! Click here to finish your order."
2. **Email 2: Overcoming Objections**
     - **Trigger**: Sent two days after Email 1 if no action has been taken.
     - **Objective**: Address potential concerns or objections that might be preventing the customer from purchasing.
     - **Content**: Include testimonials, FAQs, or additional product details to ease any doubts they may have. For example, if price is a concern, you could emphasize the value they're getting or offer a payment plan.
     - **Example CTA**: "Not sure if it's right for you? Read what other happy customers have to say!"
3. **Email 3: Final Push with a Limited-Time Offer**
     - **Trigger**: Sent three to five days after Email 2.

- **Objective**: Create urgency by offering a limited-time discount or bonus to encourage the customer to take action.
- **Content**: Highlight the offer and emphasize that it's only available for a limited time.
- **Example CTA**: "Complete your purchase today and get 10% off! Offer expires in 48 hours."

Actionable Tip: Use automated tools like Klaviyo, Mailchimp, or ActiveCampaign to set up your follow-up sequences. These platforms allow you to trigger emails based on specific actions, such as cart abandonment or an inquiry form submission.

Conclusion: Nurturing Relationships with Email Automation

Email automation is one of the most powerful tools in your marketing toolkit. By setting up **welcome series**, **nurture campaigns**, and **sales follow-up sequences**, you can build lasting relationships with your audience, provide ongoing value, and guide your subscribers toward becoming loyal customers—all with minimal effort on your part.

Whether you're just starting to build your email list or you're looking to fine-tune your existing campaigns, automation allows you to scale your email marketing efforts and deliver a personalized experience to every subscriber. By nurturing relationships over time, you'll not only increase conversions but also build a community of engaged, loyal customers who are excited to hear from you.

Now it's time to take action. Start planning your email automation sequences today and watch as your email marketing efforts begin to work for you, even while you sleep!

CHAPTER 7: LEVERAGING ONLINE COMMUNITIES AND FORUMS

In the digital age, one of the most powerful ways to grow your brand organically is by **engaging in online communities and forums**. These virtual spaces are where people come together to share knowledge, seek advice, and discuss common interests. Whether it's a niche forum, a Reddit community, or a Facebook group, online communities are hubs of engagement that present unique opportunities for small businesses to build relationships, gain visibility, and establish authority—all without spending money on ads.

In this chapter, we'll explore how you can **participate in existing communities** to extend your organic reach and how to **build your own online community** around your brand. With practical advice, real-world examples, and actionable steps, you'll learn how to tap into the power of online communities to foster genuine connections and grow your business.

Participating in Online Communities for Organic Reach

Online communities provide an excellent opportunity for businesses to engage with potential customers in an authentic way. By participating in these spaces, you can position yourself as a helpful, knowledgeable presence without coming across as overly promotional. The key is to **offer value first**—this builds trust and credibility, which can later translate into leads, referrals, and loyal customers.

Identifying Relevant Forums and Groups

The first step in leveraging online communities is identifying which ones are most relevant to your industry, target audience, and expertise. There are countless forums and groups online, so it's important to focus your efforts on the ones where your ideal customers are active.

Here are some of the most popular types of online communities:

1. Reddit

Reddit is a massive online platform that's divided into smaller communities, called **subreddits**, each focused on a specific topic. From industry-specific communities to hobbyist groups, there's a subreddit for nearly every interest imaginable.

Why Reddit is valuable for businesses:

- **Targeted communities**: You can find subreddits that are highly relevant to your niche. For example, if you run a local coffee shop, you might engage with subreddits like r/Coffee or r/CoffeeLovers to connect with passionate coffee enthusiasts.
- **High engagement**: Reddit users are often very active in discussions, making it a great platform for businesses looking to have in-depth conversations with potential customers.

Example: A fitness coach could join subreddits like r/Fitness or r/PersonalTraining and provide free advice on workout routines, nutrition, and injury prevention. By answering questions and offering tips, they can build a reputation as a knowledgeable expert and potentially attract clients.

2. Facebook Groups

Facebook Groups are another powerful tool for connecting with your audience. These groups can be public or private, and they often bring together people with shared interests, from local business communities to niche hobbyists.

Why Facebook Groups are valuable:

- **Active engagement**: Facebook Groups tend to have high levels of interaction, with members regularly posting questions, sharing advice, and discussing relevant topics.
- **Community building**: As a business owner, you can join relevant groups or create your own to foster engagement around your brand. Facebook makes it easy to share multimedia content, host live videos, and facilitate conversations.

Example: A digital marketing consultant might join a Facebook Group for small business owners and provide tips on growing their online presence. Over time, by offering valuable insights, the consultant can attract potential clients who are looking for help with their marketing strategy.

3. Industry-Specific Forums

Beyond general platforms like Reddit and Facebook, many industries have their own niche forums where professionals and enthusiasts gather to share knowledge. These forums tend to have highly engaged users who are deeply interested in the topics discussed.

Why industry-specific forums are valuable:

- **Targeted audience**: The people in these forums are often very knowledgeable and passionate about the industry, making it a great place to build relationships and establish authority.
- **Less competition**: Since these forums are often niche, there may be less competition compared to broader platforms, allowing you to stand out more easily.

Example: A graphic designer could participate in a design forum like Behance or Dribbble, where they can share their portfolio, provide feedback on others' work, and engage in discussions about design trends. This not only helps build their reputation but can also lead to freelance opportunities.

How to Provide Value and Build Authority in Online Communities

Once you've identified the right forums and groups, the next step is to **engage** with the community in a way that adds value and builds your authority. Remember, the goal isn't to sell your product or service right away—it's to become a trusted member of the community, someone people turn to for advice and insight.

Here's how to provide value and build authority:

1. Be Helpful, Not Promotional

The biggest mistake businesses make in online communities is diving in with a promotional mindset. Nobody likes to be sold to, especially in spaces where people are looking for genuine advice or connections. Instead, focus on **helping** others by answering questions, providing tips, and offering resources that align with your expertise.

Actionable Tip: If someone in a Facebook Group asks a question about how to improve their website's SEO, a web developer could offer practical advice without immediately pitching their services. By showing their expertise and being genuinely helpful, they increase the chances that the person—and others in the group—will reach out when they're ready for professional help.

2. Share Valuable Resources

One of the best ways to add value in online communities is by sharing **useful resources**. This could be anything from helpful articles and blog posts to tools, templates, or free downloads that solve common problems.

Example: A financial advisor could share a budgeting template in a personal finance subreddit, offering it for free to anyone who wants to take control of their finances. By providing a resource that's genuinely useful, they build goodwill and increase the chances of people reaching out for further financial advice.

3. Participate in Discussions and Ask Questions

Engagement is a two-way street. Don't just answer questions—ask them, too. By starting discussions or asking for advice, you can spark conversations that increase your visibility and show that you're an active, interested member of the community.

Actionable Tip: A marketing consultant could start a conversation in a small business forum, asking, "What's the biggest challenge you've faced with your digital marketing strategy this year?" This opens up a discussion where the consultant can provide insights while also learning more about the pain points of potential clients.

4. Share Your Expertise Thoughtfully

While you don't want to come across as overly self-promotional, there are ways to **share your expertise** in a way that positions you as an authority. When relevant, mention your experience or share case studies that illustrate how you've helped others in similar situations.

Example: A fitness trainer might respond to a question in a health and wellness forum by sharing a brief case study about how they helped a client lose weight using a specific workout plan. By illustrating real results, the trainer can build credibility and attract interest from other members.

Creating Your Own Online Community

While participating in existing communities is an excellent way to grow your organic reach, building your **own online community** around your brand offers even more potential. When you create a space where your audience can gather, engage, and connect, you become the leader of that community, giving you greater control over the conversations and relationships that develop.

Building and Nurturing a Community Around Your Brand

Creating an online community isn't just about gathering followers —it's about fostering meaningful connections and discussions around topics that matter to your audience. Whether it's through a Facebook Group, a private Slack channel, or a membership site, your goal is to create a space where people feel valued, heard, and eager to participate.

Here's how to build and nurture a thriving community around your brand:

1. Define Your Community's Purpose

Before creating your online community, it's important to define its purpose. What value will the community offer its members? What kind of discussions will take place? Having a clear vision will help you attract the right people and create a sense of belonging.

Example: If you run a natural skincare brand, you could create a Facebook Group dedicated to helping people achieve healthy, glowing skin using natural products. The group's purpose could be to share tips, answer questions, and discuss the benefits of natural ingredients.

2. Promote Engagement and Interaction

The key to a successful community is engagement. Encourage your members to participate by asking questions, sharing their experiences, and offering feedback. You can also post prompts, polls, and discussion starters to keep the conversation flowing.

Actionable Tip: A fitness studio could create weekly challenges in their Facebook Group, such as "Share your favorite at-home workout move" or "Post a picture of your post-workout meal." This kind of engagement keeps the community active and fosters a sense of camaraderie.

3. Host Discussions, Q&A Sessions, and Live Chats

One of the best ways to engage your community is by hosting **live events** like discussions, Q&A sessions, or live chats. These real-time interactions allow you to connect with your audience more deeply and offer immediate value.

Example: A marketing consultant could host a live Q&A session in their Facebook Group, where members can ask questions about their marketing strategies. This not only provides valuable insights but also positions the consultant as an expert in the field.

4. Provide Exclusive Content and Perks

Make your community feel special by offering **exclusive content and perks** that they can't get anywhere else. This could be early access to new products, behind-the-scenes content, or members-only discounts.

Example: A bakery could share exclusive recipes in their online community that aren't available on their website or social media.

They could also offer early access to new products or discounts for community members.

Conclusion: Building Relationships Through Online Communities

Online communities and forums are invaluable tools for businesses looking to grow their organic reach and build meaningful connections. Whether you're participating in existing groups or creating your own community, the key to success lies in **providing value** and **fostering genuine relationships**.

By becoming an active, helpful presence in the right online spaces, you can position yourself as an authority in your industry and attract loyal customers who trust your expertise. And when you take the leap to create your own community, you open the door to even deeper engagement and lasting relationships with your audience.

Now it's your turn—start identifying the communities where your audience is active, offer your expertise, and begin building a community that amplifies your brand's reach and impact.

CHAPTER 8: BUILDING PARTNERSHIPS AND COLLABORATIONS

In business, especially for small businesses, the saying "it's not what you know, but who you know" still holds significant weight. **Building partnerships and collaborations** can be a powerful way to grow your brand organically, expand your audience, and increase your influence. By forging relationships with other businesses, influencers, and thought leaders, you open the door to new opportunities and creative ways to promote your brand—often with little to no financial investment.

In this chapter, we'll explore the power of networking and collaboration, practical marketing tactics you can implement, and how to partner with local influencers to increase your organic reach. With actionable steps, real-world examples, and strategies, you'll learn how to harness the potential of partnerships to grow your business and build a supportive network that drives long-term success.

The Power of Networking and Collaboration

Networking is more than attending events and handing out business cards. It's about building **genuine relationships** with other businesses, influencers, and thought leaders who can help you grow your business while you offer value in return. Effective collaborations can open doors to new customers, new ideas, and new opportunities that you might not have achieved on your own.

Why Networking Matters for Small Businesses

For small business owners, networking offers a unique advantage: **leveraging the reach and expertise** of others. When you collaborate with another business or influencer, you're tapping into their audience and community. It's a mutually beneficial relationship where both parties grow their exposure and build credibility.

Here's why networking and collaboration are essential for small businesses:

1. **Increased Visibility**: By partnering with another business or influencer, you're introducing your brand to a new audience. When their followers see them endorsing or collaborating with you, it adds credibility to your brand.
2. **Credibility by Association**: When you collaborate with respected brands or influencers, their authority and trust extend to your business. This trust helps potential customers feel more confident in choosing your product or service.
3. **Shared Resources**: Whether it's co-hosting an event, sharing social media campaigns, or pooling together resources for a project, collaborations often allow you to access more resources than you could on your own.
4. **Innovation Through Partnership**: Working with others often sparks new ideas, innovation, and creativity. You're exposed to fresh perspectives, and these can inspire new strategies or improvements for your own business.

Building Relationships with Other Businesses, Influencers, and Thought Leaders

Building meaningful partnerships starts with **building relationships**. It's important to approach networking with a genuine mindset—looking for ways to add value to others rather than just focusing on what you can gain. Successful collaborations are always a two-way street, so your approach should be one of **mutual benefit**.

Here's how to start building these valuable relationships:

1. Identify Potential Partners

The first step is identifying businesses, influencers, or thought leaders who align with your brand values and audience. Look for those who have complementary, not competing, services or products. For example, if you own a bakery, collaborating with a local café that doesn't sell baked goods but serves your items could be a great fit.

Actionable Tip: Create a list of 10-20 businesses or influencers you admire and would like to work with. Think about what they offer and how your brand can complement their offering, whether it's by providing value to their audience or collaborating on a mutually beneficial project.

2. Build Genuine Connections

Networking isn't about making a sale right away. It's about **building relationships over time**. Start by engaging with potential partners on social media—commenting on their posts, sharing their content, and supporting their initiatives. Attend industry events, both online and in-person, where these businesses or individuals are active. Over time, these small interactions can lead to deeper conversations and eventual collaborations.

Example: A local florist could start interacting with a nearby wedding planner by commenting on their Instagram posts, sharing wedding tips, and eventually reaching out with a proposal for a collaborative bridal event.

3. Offer Value First

When approaching potential partners, lead with how you can **provide value**. Whether you're offering your expertise, sharing your audience, or contributing to a project, show that the collaboration will benefit both sides. This value-first approach builds goodwill and increases the likelihood of a successful partnership.

Actionable Tip: When reaching out to a potential partner, frame your message around what you can offer. For instance, "I admire the work you do, and I think my expertise in graphic design could be useful for an upcoming project. I'd love to collaborate on creating some visuals for your next campaign, and in exchange, I'd be happy to promote your services to my audience."

Collaborative Marketing Tactics

Now that we've discussed how to build partnerships, let's dive into specific collaborative marketing tactics that you can implement. These strategies are designed to boost visibility for both parties while providing value to each other's audiences.

Co-Hosting Events

One of the most effective ways to collaborate with another business is by **co-hosting an event**. This could be a physical event like a workshop, pop-up shop, or charity fundraiser, or it could be an online event such as a webinar or Instagram Live session.

Co-hosting events allows both businesses to pool resources, promote the event to their respective audiences, and provide a unique experience that brings their communities together.

Example: A yoga studio might team up with a local health food store to host a wellness workshop. The yoga studio could lead a mindfulness class, while the health food store provides snacks and nutritional advice. Both businesses benefit from cross-promotion and increased visibility, as they introduce each other to their customer bases.

Actionable Tip: Identify businesses that serve a similar audience and propose a co-hosted event. Make sure the event aligns with both brands and offers real value to attendees, whether it's educational, entertaining, or inspiring.

Guest Blogging

Guest blogging is a win-win for businesses looking to increase their online presence and drive traffic to their websites. It involves writing a blog post for another company's website or inviting someone to write a guest post for yours. This not only helps both businesses tap into each other's audiences but also boosts SEO through backlinks.

Example: A marketing consultant could write a guest blog post for a local business group's website on "Top 5 Marketing Tips for Small Business Owners." In return, the business group might write a post for the consultant's blog about "The Importance of Local Networking for Entrepreneurs." Both businesses benefit from new exposure and improved SEO rankings.

Actionable Tip: Reach out to businesses or influencers in your industry and offer to write a guest blog post. Make sure the content you offer is highly relevant to their audience and provides valuable insights or tips.

Cross-Promotions

Cross-promotion involves two or more businesses promoting each other's products or services to their respective audiences. This can be done through social media shoutouts, email newsletters, or even special joint promotions.

Example: A local fitness studio and a nearby smoothie shop might agree to cross-promote each other's businesses. The fitness studio could offer a discount for the smoothie shop's customers, while the smoothie shop promotes a free class pass for fitness studio attendees. This type of partnership benefits both businesses by offering added value to their customers while driving new traffic to each other.

Actionable Tip: Identify local businesses that target similar audiences and propose a cross-promotion. Start with something simple, like featuring each other's products or services on social media, and then explore other opportunities, such as offering joint discounts.

Partnering with Local Influencers for Organic Reach

Partnering with influencers—especially **local influencers**—can have a tremendous impact on your organic reach. These individuals have built a loyal following in your community, and when they promote your business, it feels more like a trusted recommendation than an ad.

Why Partner with Local Influencers?

Local influencers have built their credibility by creating content that resonates with their followers, many of whom are likely to be within your target market. By partnering with them, you can reach a **highly engaged audience** in your area without the cost of traditional advertising.

Here's why partnering with local influencers is effective:

- **Trust and Authenticity**: Influencers are trusted voices in their communities, and their followers often see their recommendations as genuine endorsements.
- **Targeted Audience**: Local influencers allow you to

reach people in your geographic area, making them ideal for brick-and-mortar businesses or service-based businesses with a local customer base.
- **Cost-Effective**: Compared to celebrity influencers, local influencers are often more affordable and open to creative collaborations, making them accessible for small businesses.

How to Collaborate with Local Influencers

1. Identify the Right Influencers

Not all influencers are created equal. The key is to partner with influencers whose followers align with your target audience. Look for local influencers with **engaged followers** who are likely to be interested in your products or services.

Actionable Tip: Use tools like Instagram or TikTok's search features to find influencers in your area who align with your brand. Look for people who post consistently and receive genuine engagement from their followers (comments, likes, shares).

2. Create a Mutually Beneficial Proposal

When reaching out to influencers, make sure you propose a collaboration that benefits both parties. Be clear about what you're offering—whether it's free products, compensation, or a revenue share—and how the collaboration will add value for their followers.

Example: A bakery might reach out to a local food influencer and offer free samples in exchange for a feature on their Instagram. The influencer could post a story or a review of the bakery, showing their followers where to find the best local treats.

3. Collaborate on Content Creation

Influencers are experts at creating engaging content, so let them take the lead in designing how they'll feature your product or service. Collaborating on content that feels natural and authentic to the influencer's audience is more likely to drive organic engagement.

Example: A boutique clothing store might partner with a local fashion influencer to create a "Spring Wardrobe Essentials" post, featuring outfits from the store. The influencer could model the clothes and create a series of Instagram posts or stories showing off their favorite pieces.

Actionable Tip: Make sure to provide influencers with creative freedom while staying aligned with your brand. Influencers know what resonates best with their followers, so trust their expertise in content creation.

Building Long-Lasting Partnerships

Collaboration and partnerships are about more than short-term gains—they're about **building long-lasting relationships** that support your business's growth over time. By networking with other businesses, thought leaders, and influencers, you create opportunities for shared success and collective growth.

Start by identifying potential partners in your community or industry, and always lead with value. Whether you're co-hosting events, cross-promoting products, or partnering with local influencers, each collaboration strengthens your brand's visibility and credibility. And as you continue to nurture these relationships, you'll build a supportive network that amplifies your marketing efforts and opens the door to new opportunities.

CHAPTER 9: ANALYZING AND MEASURING YOUR ORGANIC MARKETING SUCCESS

In the world of organic marketing, the ability to analyze and measure your success is the key to long-term growth. Creating great content, engaging with your audience, and building partnerships are all essential components of a solid marketing strategy—but without tracking and evaluating your efforts, you won't know what's truly working. That's where measurement comes in.

In this chapter, we'll explore why measurement is crucial for sustainable growth, how to focus on the right metrics, the tools available to help you track your marketing performance, and how to adjust your strategy based on what the data tells you. Whether you're looking to drive more traffic, boost engagement, or increase conversions, having a clear understanding of your metrics will help you refine your approach and maximize your organic marketing efforts.

Why Measurement is Key to Sustaining Growth

Organic marketing takes time to yield results, but when done correctly, it leads to steady, sustainable growth. To achieve this, measurement is essential because it:

- **Informs decision-making**: Knowing which tactics drive results and which don't allows you to double down on what works and cut out what doesn't.
- **Optimizes your efforts**: Tracking performance helps you make adjustments to your content, platforms, and engagement strategies in real-time, leading to better results.
- **Demonstrates ROI**: Measuring key performance indicators (KPIs) helps you understand the return on investment (ROI) for your time, energy, and resources spent on marketing.
- **Provides accountability**: By setting measurable goals and tracking progress, you can ensure that your marketing efforts align with your business objectives.

Without measurement, you might waste time on strategies that don't resonate with your audience or miss out on opportunities to improve your performance. **Data-driven decision-making** is what allows your marketing strategy to evolve and grow stronger over time.

Understanding Which Metrics Matter (Engagement, Traffic, Conversions)

With an overwhelming amount of data available, it's important to focus on the metrics that truly reflect your business's success. The right metrics can help you gauge how effective your marketing efforts are at driving traffic, engaging your audience, and converting visitors into leads or customers.

Here are the core metrics you should prioritize:

1. Engagement Metrics

Engagement metrics show how your audience interacts with your content. High engagement typically signals that your content resonates with your audience, which can boost brand loyalty and visibility.

Key engagement metrics include:

- **Likes, Shares, and Comments**: These metrics reflect how well your social media posts, blog articles, or email newsletters are performing in terms of generating conversations and interactions.
- **Click-Through Rate (CTR)**: CTR measures how many people click on links within your content, such as blog posts, emails, or social media posts, to learn more or take action.
- **Time on Site**: This metric tracks how long visitors spend on your website, blog, or specific pages. The longer they stay, the more engaged they are with your content.
- **Bounce Rate**: A high bounce rate indicates that visitors are leaving your site without exploring further, which may suggest that your content isn't meeting their expectations.

Example: A bakery might track Instagram engagement to see which types of posts (e.g., photos of new pastries or behind-the-scenes baking videos) receive the most likes, comments, and shares. This helps them understand what content their audience enjoys and engages with most.

2. Traffic Metrics

Traffic metrics give you insight into how many people are visiting your website, where they're coming from, and how they're finding you. Monitoring your traffic sources helps you determine which marketing efforts are driving the most visitors.

Key traffic metrics include:

- **Total Visits**: The number of people visiting your website in a specific time frame.
- **Traffic Sources**: This metric shows where your website visitors are coming from, including organic search (SEO), social media, referral links, or direct visits.
- **Pages per Session**: This tracks how many pages a visitor views in a single session. Higher numbers suggest that visitors are exploring more of your content, which can indicate strong engagement.

Example: A local florist could use Google Analytics to track how many visitors are coming to their website from social media platforms versus organic search. If social media is generating more traffic, they might decide to increase their content creation for those platforms.

3. Conversion Metrics

Conversion metrics are arguably the most important, as they measure the effectiveness of your marketing in turning visitors into leads or customers. Whether your goal is to increase sales, grow your email list, or get more consultation bookings, conversion metrics tell you how well your marketing efforts are driving those actions.

Key conversion metrics include:

- **Conversion Rate**: The percentage of website visitors who complete a desired action (e.g., signing up for your email list, booking a consultation, or making a purchase).
- **Lead Generation**: This tracks how many leads (e.g.,

email subscribers or form submissions) your marketing generates.
- **Sales**: For eCommerce businesses, tracking sales is essential to measure the financial success of your campaigns.

Example: A local yoga studio might run a campaign promoting a free class for first-time visitors. By tracking how many people sign up for the free class through their website, the studio can determine how well their marketing efforts are converting traffic into new clients.

Tools for Tracking Organic Marketing Performance

You don't have to track your metrics manually—there are plenty of tools available that help you analyze and measure your marketing performance. These tools provide valuable data about your website traffic, social media engagement, and email marketing campaigns, giving you a clear picture of what's working and what needs improvement.

Here are the key tools you can use:

1. Google Analytics

Google Analytics is a must-have tool for tracking website traffic and user behavior. It offers comprehensive insights into how visitors find your website, how they interact with it, and what actions they take.

Key features include:

- **Audience Insights**: Learn about your visitors' demographics, interests, and geographic locations.
- **Acquisition Reports**: Discover which channels (organic search, social media, referrals) are driving the most traffic to your site.

- **Behavior Reports**: Track what pages your visitors are viewing, how long they stay on your site, and where they drop off.
- **Conversion Tracking**: Set up goals to track conversions like form submissions, purchases, or email sign-ups.

Actionable Tip: Set up Google Analytics goals that align with your business objectives, such as tracking how many visitors sign up for your newsletter or make a purchase.

2. Social Media Insights

Social media platforms like Facebook, Instagram, and Twitter offer built-in **analytics tools** that allow you to track your social media performance. These tools provide data on audience engagement, reach, and growth, helping you understand how well your posts resonate with followers.

Key metrics include:

- **Engagement**: Likes, comments, shares, and click-through rates give you insight into how well your content connects with your audience.
- **Follower Growth**: Monitor your follower count over time to see how your audience is expanding.
- **Reach and Impressions**: These metrics show how many people are seeing your posts and how often your content appears in their feeds.

Example: A boutique clothing store might use Instagram Insights to track how often their posts are saved or shared. If behind-the-scenes fashion tips generate high engagement, they can focus on creating more of this content.

3. Email Marketing Platforms

If you use email marketing tools like **Mailchimp**, **Constant Contact**, or **Klaviyo**, these platforms provide detailed analytics on how your subscribers engage with your emails.

Key email metrics include:

- **Open Rate**: The percentage of subscribers who open your emails.
- **Click-Through Rate (CTR)**: The percentage of subscribers who click on links within your email.
- **Unsubscribe Rate**: The number of people who opt-out of your email list after receiving a campaign.

Actionable Tip: Test different subject lines, email designs, and calls-to-action using A/B testing to see what resonates best with your audience. Use the data to optimize future email campaigns.

How to Adjust Your Strategy Based on Results

Data analysis is only valuable if you use it to **inform your strategy**. Once you've gathered insights from your analytics, you'll need to adjust your marketing tactics to enhance what's working and fix what isn't.

Identifying What's Working and What's Not

Start by identifying your most successful campaigns and tactics. Look for patterns in the data to understand what's driving engagement, traffic, and conversions. Here's how to break it down:

- **Which platforms perform best?**: Identify whether social media, email marketing, or organic search is driving the most traffic and conversions.
- **Which content resonates?**: Examine which types of content (e.g., blog posts, videos, infographics) generate

the highest engagement. Are there specific topics that consistently outperform others?
- **Are there underperforming areas?**: Pinpoint campaigns, platforms, or types of content that aren't meeting expectations and consider how you can improve them.

Iterating on Content and Engagement Tactics for Better Results

Once you've identified what works, focus on **iterating** to improve your results. This means experimenting with new strategies, testing different types of content, and refining your tactics based on performance.

Here's how to refine your strategy:

1. Experiment with Content Formats

If certain types of content are driving engagement, experiment with new formats to enhance your results. For example:

- Turn a popular blog post into a video or infographic.
- Repurpose a high-engagement social media post into an email newsletter.
- Try new formats like live videos, polls, or user-generated content.

2. Personalize Your Marketing

If your audience responds well to personalized content, focus on segmenting your email list or creating targeted social media campaigns. By tailoring your message to specific segments, you can improve engagement and conversion rates.

Example: An online shoe retailer might create separate email campaigns for men's and women's shoes based on customer preferences, increasing the relevance of each campaign.

3. Test and Optimize

Regularly test new tactics to see what works best for your audience. For instance, you can:

- **A/B test** different subject lines or email designs.
- Experiment with new posting times on social media.
- Create new calls-to-action to see which drive more conversions.

Actionable Tip: Set aside time each month to review your analytics and test new ideas. Use data-driven insights to optimize your marketing efforts continually.

Using Data to Drive Success

Measuring and analyzing your organic marketing success is the key to growth. By tracking the right metrics, using powerful tools like Google Analytics and social media insights, and refining your strategy based on data, you'll build a marketing plan that evolves and improves over time.

Remember, organic marketing is a long-term game. Continuous measurement, iteration, and optimization will help you create more impactful campaigns that drive engagement, traffic, and conversions. As you grow more familiar with your audience's preferences and behavior, you'll be able to make smarter decisions that lead to sustainable, lasting success for your business.

CHAPTER 10: SCALING YOUR ORGANIC MARKETING OVER TIME

You've laid the groundwork for a successful organic marketing strategy—now it's time to think about **scaling** those efforts. Scaling your organic marketing means growing your reach, building a loyal customer base, and driving more conversions, all without dramatically increasing your marketing budget. The key to scaling organically lies in being strategic, consistent, and focused on sustainable growth that aligns with your brand's long-term vision.

In this chapter, we'll explore how to **strategically grow your organic marketing** efforts over time, build a loyal customer base, and expand your reach while keeping costs low. We'll also discuss **sustainable growth strategies**, helping you stay consistent with your marketing efforts, balance long-term brand-building with short-term goals, and ensure your marketing strategy continues to evolve as your business grows.

Growing Your Organic Efforts Strategically

Scaling your organic marketing doesn't happen overnight—it's a process that requires careful planning, experimentation, and adaptation. By focusing on **strategic growth**, you can expand your reach, increase engagement, and grow your business without significantly increasing your marketing spend.

Building a Loyal Customer Base Over Time

One of the most valuable assets a small business can cultivate is a **loyal customer base**. Loyal customers don't just make repeat purchases—they become advocates for your brand, sharing their positive experiences with others and driving word-of-mouth growth.

Here's how you can build loyalty and foster strong relationships with your audience:

1. Deliver Consistent Value

Your organic marketing efforts should always provide value to your audience, whether through educational content, entertainment, or exclusive offers. The more valuable your content is, the more likely your audience will stay engaged and loyal over time.

Example: A fitness coach could offer regular tips, workout plans, and healthy recipes to their audience via a blog or email newsletter. By consistently providing valuable information that helps their audience reach their goals, they build trust and loyalty.

2. Engage and Connect Personally

Building a personal connection with your audience is critical to fostering loyalty. Take time to engage with your followers on social media, reply to comments, and show that you care about their experiences. Personalization is another powerful way to connect—tailoring content and offers based on their preferences or behaviors can significantly increase loyalty.

Actionable Tip: Send personalized thank-you emails or offer exclusive discounts to repeat customers. Small gestures of appreciation can make a big difference in building long-term relationships.

3. Create a Community Around Your Brand

A strong community creates a sense of belonging, turning casual customers into passionate brand advocates. Encourage interaction between your audience members, whether through social media groups, online forums, or events, and foster a space where people feel connected to both your brand and each other.

Example: A natural skincare brand could create a Facebook group where customers can share their skincare journeys, ask questions, and exchange tips. The brand can facilitate discussions and share behind-the-scenes content, nurturing a loyal and engaged community.

Expanding Your Reach Without Increasing Your Budget

Scaling your organic marketing doesn't mean you need to start spending more money. In fact, the beauty of organic marketing is that it allows you to expand your reach through **creativity, consistency, and community-building** rather than through expensive paid ads.

Here's how you can grow your reach without blowing your budget:

1. Leverage User-Generated Content

User-generated content (UGC) is a powerful way to expand your reach organically. When your customers create and share content featuring your brand, it serves as authentic social proof, reaching their networks and amplifying your message. Plus, it saves you the time and effort of creating all your content.

Example: A restaurant might encourage customers to share photos of their meals on Instagram with a branded hashtag, offering a chance to be featured on the restaurant's social media page. This not only provides the restaurant with free, authentic content but also extends its reach to new potential customers.

2. Partner with Micro-Influencers

Influencer marketing doesn't have to be expensive. **Micro-influencers**—individuals with smaller but highly engaged followings—are often more affordable and can deliver impressive results. By partnering with local or niche influencers who align with your brand, you can tap into their audience and gain visibility without spending big on large-scale influencer campaigns.

Actionable Tip: Offer micro-influencers free products or services in exchange for an honest review or a social media shoutout. Look for influencers whose followers match your target audience and who have strong engagement rates.

3. Optimize Your Content for SEO

Search engine optimization (SEO) is a cornerstone of organic marketing and can help you attract more visitors to your website without increasing your budget. As you scale, focus on creating **evergreen content**—high-quality, value-driven content that continues to attract traffic over time. Additionally, keep refining your keyword strategy to target terms that are relevant to your audience.

Example: A small business that sells eco-friendly cleaning products might create blog posts with SEO-optimized titles like "Top 10 Tips for Eco-Friendly Home Cleaning." Over time, these posts can rank higher in search results, driving consistent traffic to the website.

Sustainable Growth Strategies

To successfully scale your organic marketing efforts, you need to adopt strategies that are sustainable over the long term. This means focusing on consistency, aligning your marketing with your long-term brand goals, and finding the right balance between immediate wins and long-term brand-building.

How to Stay Consistent with Your Organic Marketing

Consistency is one of the most important factors in scaling organic marketing. The more consistently you deliver value, engage with your audience, and create content, the more likely your efforts will pay off in the long run.

Here's how to stay consistent:

1. Develop a Content Calendar

One of the best ways to stay consistent is by planning your content in advance. A content calendar allows you to schedule blog posts, social media updates, email campaigns, and other content around key dates, promotions, or themes. This keeps you organized and ensures you're regularly producing fresh, relevant content for your audience.

Actionable Tip: Use tools like Trello, Asana, or Google Sheets to create a simple content calendar. Plan at least a month ahead, ensuring a steady flow of content across your marketing channels.

2. Automate What You Can

Automation is your best friend when it comes to staying consistent with organic marketing. Email automation, social media scheduling, and content management tools allow you to post regularly without having to manually create and publish content in real-time.

Example: A local spa could set up an automated email series for new subscribers, sending a welcome message, tips for self-care, and promotional offers over the first few weeks. This ensures consistent communication without requiring constant attention.

3. Repurpose Content

Repurposing existing content allows you to get more mileage out of your work while keeping your marketing fresh. For example, a well-performing blog post can be turned into an infographic, video, or series of social media posts. Repurposing also allows you to share content across multiple platforms, reaching different segments of your audience.

Example: If you've written a blog post about "5 Tips for Starting a Garden," you could turn it into an infographic for Pinterest, a short video for Instagram Reels, or a series of tweets for Twitter. This way, you maximize the reach and impact of one piece of content.

Balancing Long-Term Brand-Building with Short-Term Goals

As you scale your organic marketing, it's essential to find the right balance between **long-term brand-building** and achieving **short-term goals**. While it's important to drive immediate results like sales or lead generation, your marketing efforts should also focus on building a lasting brand that stands the test of time.

Here's how to strike that balance:

1. Focus on Brand Storytelling

Brand storytelling is one of the most effective ways to build a strong, enduring brand. By sharing the story behind your business, your mission, and the values that guide you, you can create an emotional connection with your audience that goes beyond a single transaction. Storytelling helps you cultivate brand loyalty and build a community around your business.

Actionable Tip: Regularly share stories that highlight your brand's journey, your team's experiences, or your customers' success stories. This can be done through blog posts, email newsletters, or social media updates.

2. Set SMART Goals

When scaling your marketing efforts, it's important to set both **short-term and long-term goals**. Using the SMART framework—**Specific, Measurable, Achievable, Relevant, Time-bound**—can help you stay focused on what matters. Make sure your goals are realistic and align with both immediate needs (like generating leads) and your long-term vision (like becoming a leader in your industry).

Example: A short-term goal might be "Increase email list subscribers by 10% in the next three months," while a long-term goal could be "Establish our brand as the top sustainable fashion retailer in our city within two years."

3. Monitor and Adapt

As you scale, it's essential to regularly monitor your progress and adapt your strategies based on the data you collect. Track your key performance indicators (KPIs) to measure success and make adjustments as needed to stay on course for long-term growth.

Actionable Tip: Set up monthly or quarterly reviews of your marketing metrics. Use tools like Google Analytics, social media insights, or email platform reports to track engagement, traffic, and conversions. Use this data to refine your strategy and keep growing.

Scaling with Purpose and Strategy

Scaling your organic marketing is about growing strategically and sustainably. By building a loyal customer base, expanding your reach creatively, and staying consistent, you'll set the stage for long-term success. As you scale, always keep your brand's long-term vision in mind while pursuing short-term goals. Whether it's engaging with your community, optimizing your content for SEO, or leveraging partnerships, the key is to remain flexible, data-driven, and focused on delivering value.

Building a Long-Lasting Brand through Organic Marketing

Organic marketing isn't just a set of tactics—it's a **long-term investment** in your brand's future. For small businesses, it's one of the most powerful ways to build sustainable growth without relying on hefty advertising budgets. By focusing on authenticity, creating value-driven content, and nurturing real connections with your audience, organic marketing enables you to build a brand that resonates deeply with customers and stands the test of time.

The Importance of Organic Marketing for Sustainable Growth

Organic marketing is about more than just driving traffic or increasing sales. It's about **building trust, credibility, and loyalty** over time. While paid ads can deliver quick results, organic marketing builds a foundation for **sustainable growth** that lasts. When you focus on organic efforts—whether through SEO, social media, email marketing, or partnerships—you're creating a brand that's genuine, approachable, and memorable.

Organic marketing encourages businesses to:

- **Focus on providing value**: Create content that educates, inspires, or entertains your audience, offering them something meaningful in return for their time and attention.
- **Build relationships**: By engaging authentically with your audience, you foster deeper connections that lead to customer loyalty and word-of-mouth growth.
- **Grow strategically**: Organic marketing is scalable. As your brand grows, your organic marketing efforts evolve alongside it, expanding your reach and influence naturally.

Start Small, Stay Consistent, and Measure Results

The journey of organic marketing starts small but can lead to significant, lasting results. If you're new to organic marketing or just beginning your efforts, don't be overwhelmed by the scope. Start by focusing on a few key tactics—whether it's optimizing your website for search engines, building a presence on one or two social media platforms, or starting an email newsletter.

The key to success is **consistency**. Keep showing up, creating content, and engaging with your audience, even when progress feels slow. Organic marketing takes time, but the results are worth the effort.

As you grow, it's important to **measure your success**. Track your key metrics—engagement, traffic, and conversions—to see what's working and where you can improve. Use this data to refine your strategy and continue scaling your efforts over time.

Building Meaningful, Lasting Relationships

At the heart of organic marketing is the goal of building meaningful relationships with your customers. People want to support brands they feel connected to—brands that share their values, understand their needs, and engage with them on a personal level. By focusing on these relationships, you create a community of loyal customers who trust your brand, advocate for it, and return time and time again.

Whether through storytelling, personalized content, or simply showing up for your audience consistently, organic marketing helps you build those lasting connections that drive long-term success.

Inspiration for Small Businesses: Start your organic marketing journey today, knowing that the small steps you take now will lead to big, meaningful outcomes. Stay patient, stay consistent, and always keep your focus on delivering value to your audience. In doing so, you'll build a brand that not only grows but thrives, thanks to the power of authentic, relationship-driven marketing.

www.ingramcontent.com/pod-product-compliance
Lightning Source LLC
Chambersburg PA
CBHW070146230526
45471CB00002B/535